Jennifer Saunders

The Biography

Jennifer Saunders

The Biography

Jacky Hyams

metro

Published by Metro Publishing
An imprint of John Blake Publishing Ltd
3 Bramber Court, 2 Bramber Road,
London W14 9PB, England

www.johnblakepublishing.co.uk

www.facebook.com/Johnblakepub   facebook

twitter.com/johnblakepub   twitter

First published in hardback in 2012

ISBN: 978 1 85782 682 1

British Library Cataloguing-in-Publication Data:

A catalogue record for this book is available from the British Library.

LONDON BOROUGH OF WANDSWORTH		
9030 00002 8404 2		
Askews & Holts	11-Oct-2012	
920 SAUN	£17.99	
	WWX0010010/0194	

Design by www.envydesign.co.uk

Printed and bound in Great Britain by CPI Group (UK) Ltd

1 3 5 7 9 10 8 6 4 2

© Text copyright Jacky Hyams 2012

Papers used by John Blake Publishing are natural, recyclable
products made from wood grown in sustainable forests.
The manufacturing processes conform to the environmental
regulations of the country of origin.

Every attempt has been made to contact the relevant copyright-
holders, but some were unobtainable. We would be grateful
if the appropriate people could contact us.

CONTENTS

INTRODUCTION

We're watching a movie. It's the opening shot. The words appear on the screen: London, autumn, 1980. Early evening. The camera is tracking down a narrow, dingy passageway in Soho in the heart of London's West End, just a short stroll from theatreland's Shaftesbury Avenue. A brightly lit sign at the entrance to the Raymond Revue Bar declaims: 'World Centre of Erotic Entertainment'. This is an upmarket strip club, albeit the most famous and successful of its day.

A young woman, average height, early twenties, fairish hair gelled and scraped back, clad all in black, is climbing a narrow stairway inside the Revue Bar, followed by a slightly shorter friend, also in black. They're laughing, wisecracking to each other as they negotiate the stairs, en route to a small theatre right at the top of the building.

One girl works by day as a schoolteacher, the other is, in acting parlance, a 'resting' graduate, doing odd jobs between stints on the dole. What do they hope to find at the top of the stairs?

Welcome to showbiz, girls. It's 15 years later and the camera reveals a posh west London street, lots of big white houses. A Rolls-Royce pulls up at the kerb. Out totters an overdressed 40-something woman in garish, expensive designer gear, big hair framing her face, teetering unsteadily on ridiculously perilous snakeskin stilettos, half-cut, mobile in one hand, ciggy in the other, screeching giddy nonsense at the top of her voice. A somewhat extreme parody of a middle-class, social-climbing PR woman turned daft fashion victim with a perennial hangover (and a sensible, sober daughter called Saffy in a state of permanent disgust), a batty PA called Bubble and an outrageous sidekick – a blonde, beehived, vampish maghag well past her sell-by date but as sozzled and predatory as any ageing party girl who ever hailed a cab outside Harvey Nicks.

Those two young women scaling the strip-club stairs are not, of course, wannabe strippers or performers of erotic entertainment. They are Dawn French and Jennifer Saunders, heading for their first ever audition as a double act at what became the springboard for their respective glittering careers in comedy, Peter Richardson's fabled *Comic Strip*, an early 1980s launch pad for so many other stars in the comic firmament. And, of course, the screeching harridan in the Roller barely needs any introduction: the whole world knows Edina Monsoon, star of TV's *Absolutely Fabulous*, written, performed and created by

Jennifer Saunders, now one of the planet's most successful comic writers/performers.

Who can forget the shambolic adventures and riotous caricatures of *Absolutely Fabulous*, or *Ab Fab* as it became known? The seminal television series reshaped the face of British TV comedy, attained cult status globally and drew an enormous, loyal BBC following: an over-the-top celebration of Brit ladette culture, born in the early 1990s into a recession-bound Britain in desperate need of a laugh.

Such is *Absolutely Fabulous'* legendary draw and massive following, the show lives on: brand-new special episodes were created for 2011 and 2012, timed to celebrate *Ab Fab*'s twentieth anniversary, certainly, but an opportunity for a new generation of Saffys to despair at their middle-aged mums' excesses.

Yet the genesis of *Ab Fab* came from another world, from a far-off time.

When Edina exploded into British lives, a man called John Major sat in Downing Street. Interest rates were shooting up to an alarming 15 per cent. The Prince and Princess of Wales had split up, the beginning of the unfolding tragedy that led to the death of Princess Diana. Fergie was sucking toes and garnering freebies. Even the Queen owned up to her first *annus horribilis*.

With superb timing, the 1992 antics of Patsy, Edina and co. lightened the British gloom – and became the first ever TV comedy series since *Fawlty Towers* to weave its way into everyday British life and water-cooler chatter.

Call it what you will – social satire, the baby boomer generation of older women behaving beyond badly, venomous parody – there's no questioning its impact on the national psyche. And on the millions around the world who fell about laughing at Edina and associates. And incredibly... they're still laughing.

But, if anything, the revisiting of the unforgettable *Ab Fab* only serves to focus on the enduring talents of Jennifer Saunders, who has, of course, written and created a whole host of comic characters before and since the *Ab Fab* era.

Since those early days as one half of Britain's best-loved comic pairing, French and Saunders, Jennifer Saunders' career, now spanning over 30 years, has taken her right to the very peak of the entertainment industry.

Very few British female performers, aside from Dawn French, can emulate her CV, mainly because Jennifer Saunders' talents are so wide-ranging. She writes. She produces. She directs. She acts. She sings. She is the great parodist, a Sheridan for the times, sending up virtually everything: the glitterati of showbiz, the fame game itself, the ageing woman's obsession with youth, the darker vices of the media world, the excesses of cinema, pop culture – you name it, she's there, lampooning it, puncturing pretension, ridiculing pomposity.

Yet when we laugh at her creations, as is frequently the case with successful comedy, we're often laughing at ourselves, our own foibles or weaknesses, too. And because so many performers and celebrities from Lulu, to Kate Moss, to The Spice Girls, adore what Jennifer does and love to perform alongside her in the slipstream of her wit and parody, we, the audience, might even start to feel that her comic genius is giving us an insider's peek into the show business bubble.

That's an amazingly clever feat in itself. But it's even more incredible when you consider that Jennifer Saunders is an entertainer with a global audience who has flatly refused, from day one, to deploy her fame and celebrity for their own sake.

She works hard at her craft – though she has admitted, time and again, that it's very much an eleventh-hour, seat-of-the-pants spurt of intense energy that is her working style, rather than a slow, careful, measured approach to the business of comedy – and she uses her amazingly forensic observational skills to this end. She attends the key events: the first nights, the fundraising dos. Intensely loyal to her close-knit group of friends, she's always there to support them publicly if the occasion demands it. She allows herself to be photographed with her family around her. And that's it.

The consummate professional, she will be interviewed by the press and submit to the endless rounds of questions when the time comes to promote her work because that is part of the entertainer's job.

But she firmly refuses – and has done so right from the very beginning – to allow the personal, the private, the 'this is me and my wonderful life' type of exposure that so many other well known names use, with increasing fervour, to have any place in her world. It's no secret that she's an incredibly private individual. And such is the loyalty and esteem that her closest friends and colleagues, in and out of the business, feel for her that they effectively form a protective carapace around her.

And yet the fact that there is this tight, protective circle around her, preventing any intrusion, reveals something important about Jennifer Saunders: these protectors are people who know and love her, both the woman and the work.

We are not talking about a paid team of public relations people and self-important professional gatekeepers, clipboard Nazis attending to her every whim, Hollywood style. Even amongst the tightly-knit but often bitchy world of television programme makers, for instance, it is widely acknowledged that the off-camera Jennifer Saunders is a true, kind, loyal, warm (and very witty) friend to those working alongside her.

Dawn French, so closely connected with her for so long, says this at considerable length in her own book, *Dear Fatty*, lovingly addressed to Jennifer. Yet Jennifer would never attempt to tell us such things about herself. She might make dry cracks about it all in her impeccably accented drawl, but parade herself around the world as a high achiever? Never.

Her success has brought her considerable wealth – estimates vary but there are suggestions of millions in double figures – but you won't hear her boasting about it. She openly loves the good things in life – fast cars and horse riding are her passions – the English countryside is an enduring love, and she's generous with her time when it comes to deploying her celebrity to help the less advantaged. But she won't be in our faces, endlessly telling us all about it. Ever.

It's just not her style. Once you attempt to separate the private Jennifer Saunders from any of her hugely successful, outrageous comic creations, you find the very opposite of a larger-than-life, flamboyant or excessive person like Edina Monsoon or the aptly named Vivienne Vyle, two of the many characters she has created and portrayed so brilliantly. As a result, Jennifer Saunders remains very much an enigma. A role model to millions. And, it must be said, an alluring object of desire for the opposite sex: male interviewers consistently comment on her good looks. Men admire her, women want to emulate her; it's been that way right from the start.

But the real Jennifer is resolutely obscure, hidden from view. Even that other much-loved actor and collaborator in the *Ab Fab* phenomenon Joanna Lumley has admitted that at their first meeting she thought Jennifer seemed 'intimidatingly opaque'.

Yet the things we do know about Jennifer give us some sense of her true persona. Born in July, astrologers might say she is a true Cancerian – home and family life are close to her heart and usually take priority over everything else. This is a woman who prizes stability, continuity, the traditions of country life, and small, close-knit communities. Yet she's equally at ease in a more urban, sophisticated setting: shopping for food in London's ultra-fashionable Marylebone High Street, getting behind the wheel of a super-fast sports car, soaking up the sun in Italy's most glamorous resorts.

She's been happily married to the same man, another comic genius, Adrian Edmondson, for well over a quarter of a century, quite rare in a country where one marriage in three ends in divorce and in an industry where relationships often last as long as the cameras are rolling. The Edmondsons have three daughters: two have started to make their name as performers and one is heading for a career as a fashion designer – creativity and making people laugh are the family businesses.

Yet while the pair have raised their family comfortably, dividing their time between the demands of work in London and an idyllic country sprawl in Devon, there hasn't been an excess of glitz surrounding their girls' upbringing: it's an oft-repeated legend that, at one point, one of their daughters came home from school and said accusingly to her mum: 'Are you Jennifer Saunders?'

However, in a career that took off in the far-off days of punk and continues to thrive in the iPad era, Jennifer's very obvious reluctance to self-promote and her low-key, wry approach to such a stellar, successful career are remarkable. Jennifer Saunders remains one of the funniest, most entertaining women in Britain. But she isn't going to run around reminding us.

This might be extremely frustrating for the interviewer seeking a torrent of fresh personal revelations, but in the self-obsessed world we now live in, her sangfroid is admirable. Her philosophy, virtually since day one, seems to be: good work, family, loyalty and laughter are what matters, not fame or 24/7 exposure. If you have a good time at work – and there are good times galore, creating comedy and mayhem with a team of like-minded talents – and if what you create makes other people laugh too, you're ahead of the game.

'My job is wonderful and I don't know where else I'd fit

in. It's all about having a good time, making the funniest programme you can and earning a living. It's certainly not about being famous,' she has admitted.

So where do they come from, the outward detachment and the ability to stand back from the brouhaha surrounding telly and showbiz? There are small but significant clues. Part of the skill of any comic performer or actor is their ability to observe and dissect the little nuances of human behaviour that most of us might miss or overlook.

In Jennifer's case, this all started at a very early age. As a child, for instance, she has confessed to being a bit of a starer – a quiet kid who watched others and took mental notes.

'My mother says I had to be taken away in restaurants because I'd be standing in front of tables just looking at people,' Jennifer once revealed.

Dawn French, writing in her memoir *Dear Fatty* ('Fatty' is her nickname for Jennifer), has also paid tribute to Jennifer's outward detachment or cool, which conceals the brilliance of her observation.

'She is constantly running a cynical, internal parallel tape of her real life, what she sees, hears, reads, eats, loves and hates, and it never ceases to amuse her.

'It's this sharp skill of observation that gives her the comedy spurs she uses to jolt her mind on from a trot to a canter when she is improvising or writing. On the surface, though, all is calm.'

It is, of course, a traditional English trait to be reserved or self-effacing. Understatement is the name of the game, the hallmark of being... well, terribly British. The daughter of a former RAF Group Captain, she has her own take on this:

'The big, overriding thing in our family was that any kind of taking yourself seriously was the biggest crime; you just didn't do that. My dad said: "Be serious but never take yourself seriously."'

So there it is: a very big showbiz career, a close-knit family life that means everything to her, and an inability to emote or show off in person, no matter how flamboyant her comic creations, and you start to have a sense of the somewhat reticent but outrageously gifted Jennifer Saunders.

Another important key to her real-life personality is that in times of adversity she refuses to make a big fuss: a recent bout of breast cancer was, typically, coped with quietly and as far from the public gaze as possible, until the time was appropriate to reveal what had happened. All conducted with total discretion.

'How she managed to keep her illness under wraps in an industry that is so gossipy is massive,' observed one seasoned TV writer.

The media thrives on gossip: 'Every stylist, every makeup artist, every person working in the studio tells everyone else stuff, no matter who it is. The way she managed to keep it quiet until after her treatment and recovery is incredible, but she's earned that kind of privacy. The fact that she has never used her fame in any way meant that, when the time came, everyone around her wanted to close ranks and protect her.'

Unknowable, cool, hugely attractive at every stage of her life and so very, very English, Jennifer Saunders continues to fascinate audiences of all ages around the world. It's fair to say, too, that part of that fascination is probably derived from her enigmatic persona. Twenty-first-century celebrities who sign up for limited verbal exposure – Kate Moss is a very good example – create a mystique all their own, whether deliberately or not.

This book will pay tribute to Jennifer Saunders' talents and tells her story right from the beginning. This is not a heartbreak tale of someone from the back streets who had to claw their way to the top – to discover, when they got there, that they couldn't cope with the pressures of fame. Nor is it a story about overnight success.

Jennifer Saunders' story is a tale of a shy, quiet middle-class English girl from a pleasant, rural background without any driving ambition to make herself known or forge a successful career as an entertainer. Until, by sheer chance, she spots an ad in a paper and finds herself climbing the narrow stairs of that strip club, in London's Soho – the clichéd first step, if you like, on the ladder of success.

Those who deliberately seek out celebrity for its own sake are everywhere these days, popping up with alarming regularity. Some big show business names become so hooked on their own fame or image that they can't help but rush to expose themselves to the public glare even if they don't really need to, because... well, that's what they do. Without it, they might feel their very identity is under question.

That's never going to be the case for Jennifer Saunders. She loves what she does, she knows exactly who she is and she closely guards the world she truly values. And she has learned, over time, to maintain her balance on that paper-thin line between exposure and privacy; a pragmatic showbiz insider who has never been afraid to ridicule the entertainment world's excesses, she will continue to be a private person in a very public setting. But she is a star – and she remains a star to her many millions of admirers.

What follows, in this book, is an attempt to look at her life and times – and learn something more about the woman behind the enigma.

CHAPTER 1

BEGINNINGS

Cheshire, in the north of England, is one of the country's most beautiful counties. Tiny, picturesque, 'blink and you might miss it' rural villages where time seems to have stood still. Small communities taking pride in maintaining their annual 'best-kept village in Cheshire' status. Big landowners. Farms. True blue Conservative – and likely to stay that way.

On the north Cheshire boundary lie small rural areas just outside the town of Northwich; villages such as Hartford, Weaverham, Cuddington, Acton Bridge and Crowton; pretty, mostly flat country just a short drive away from Cheshire's biggest woodland area, Delamere Forest, popular with horse riders and cyclists and a haven for wildlife. The area around here is not as flashy or bling as the money-belt Cheshire suburbs of Prestbury or Wilmslow with their expensive footballers' homes, but,

1

nonetheless, this is a desirable place for anyone to grow up in.

This rural, bucolic area, around Crowton and Acton Bridge, is where Jennifer Saunders spent her early teenage years. Until the age of 11, she would lead a peripatetic life with her parents and three brothers. Her father's career as an officer in the RAF took the Saunders family all over the country, and, at one point, overseas to Cyprus and Turkey for short periods of time.

Jennifer's mother, Jane, like all the other RAF officers' wives bringing up their children on RAF bases or stations, would have become accustomed to having to move frequently and to swapping one family home for another, the usual upheavals and changes involved in a post-war RAF life of two-year, or even shorter, postings.

Nowadays, provision is frequently made for officers' children to be sent off to boarding school. Back then, however, it was often the case that children lived on or around the base and had to make the best of the 'chopping and changing' situation, adjusting to each new move and set of faces as they came along, yet always armed with the knowledge that they would be moving on again soon anyway.

So as a Forces child, Jennifer went to many different primary schools. And over time she developed her own coping mechanism for always being 'the new girl', often arriving at the new school just a little bit later than the others.

'It was never at the beginning of term, always midway,' she recalled in an interview with *The Sunday Times*

Magazine in August 2007. 'So you'd work out where to sit. You'd think: "Oh that's that kind of gang, that's that one. Why is there a place left next to this person?" You learn to observe and fit in without being noticed. Odd, as I've chosen this career.'

Jennifer Jane Saunders was born in Sleaford Maternity Hospital, Lincolnshire, in July 1958. Her family was based in the area during her father's posting to nearby RAF Cranwell, one of the RAF's largest officer training units.

Each step up the RAF career ladder for Jennifer's father meant another posting, a fresh move. And he had a very successful career until 1970, when Group Captain Robert Thomas Saunders (known to friends as 'Tom') left the RAF for good to step back into civilian life and a job with British Aerospace. Only then could Jennifer's family settle down permanently into life in a rambling Victorian house in rural Acton Bridge. And her mother, Jane, began working as a teacher at The Grange, a private day school in the nearby village of Hartford.

Curiously enough, this background as an Air Force child is something Jennifer has in common with some of the most significant people in her adult life: Dawn French's father was an RAF sergeant; *Absolutely Fabulous* close cohort Joanna Lumley's father, a major in the Gurkha Rifles, was posted to Kashmir in India, where Joanna was born; and, perhaps most significantly, the father of her future husband, Adrian Edmondson, was a teacher working for the British Army and the RAF.

Sheer coincidence or a bond shared with those who had also known a childhood constantly on the move? It's difficult to be certain. But Jennifer has never denied the fact that moving around all the time as a child did help with her powers of observation as a comic writer and actor.

'You do learn how to fit in quite well. A lot of that is just watching. And actually not having much of a personality,' she told the *Guardian* in June 2004.

'I think you develop a knack, so you become quite self-contained. I had a very happy home life; I don't remember anything being traumatic,' she revealed to the *Liverpool Daily Post* in an interview a few years later.

In 1969, with the family settled in the Cheshire country-side, Jennifer was sent to a local grammar school, Northwich County Grammar School for Girls in Leftwich, just south of the town of Northwich.

At the time, many people in the Northwich area worked for the former ICI (Imperial Chemical Industries), which had offices and industrial plants nearby. Some of Jennifer's classmates were the children of ICI staff, bright working-class kids who had passed the 11-plus exam. Even in the late 1960s, Northwich County was a very strictly-run girls' school, a 1950s-style educational establishment governed on old-fashioned, super-strict lines. The peace and love revolution might have started elsewhere, but at Northwich County, with 1,000 girls completing their secondary education, revolution and rebellion were definitely not running amok.

'You had to wear gym shorts six inches above the knee,' recollected one former pupil of the time.

The schoolgirls' navy blue uniform included a maroon beret. 'If you were caught without it, you had to wear it in school all day. The head and her associate would drive around the local bus station spotting beret-less heads.'

Girls attending Northwich County at the time recall a disciplinarian running the school: a headmistress with a scary reputation. There were rumours of corporal punishment. And there were frequent stories of teachers being seen leaving the head's office in floods of tears.

'Whatever you did, you were in the wrong as far as she was concerned,' remembered another ex-pupil.

Oh dear. You can picture a 13-year-old Jennifer in her school uniform: navy pinafore dress to the knee with white shirt and red tie, sitting in class, staring out of the window, bored out of her mind with it all – but not daring to react against the day-to-day discipline with rebellion or cheek. Definitely not a wild child.

'I was an apathetic, quiet kid – that's how I'd have described myself,' recalled Jennifer of those early years to *More* magazine.

'I wasn't interested in much at school – except biology. I liked dissecting! It was an all-girls school so the only flirtations with boys were on the bus. And they were just embarrassing.'

'I used to be very shy which exhibited itself in morose, non-communicative behaviour,' she admitted to the *Sunday Express*. 'I grew up thinking whatever I said would sound stupid. So you end up saying nothing.'

'I was into horses and the occasional disco,' she told *Tatler*. 'It wasn't like I had lots of friends around. I would love to have been wild, but I could never do it. I never got into drugs or anything. I could never lose control.

'I hardly raised my eyes. I was endlessly blushing. It was biological. I just didn't want the attention, but I daydreamed a lot.'

'I was mad on horses. Completely,' she revealed in a BBC Radio 4 interview with Sue Lawley for *Desert Island Discs* in December 1996.

'My big ambition was to become a three-day eventer until I was about 16.

I got my first pony in Wiltshire – I had a friend who had a farm.'

Her school reports tended to be of the 'could try harder' variety. Yet there was one area where Jennifer's teenage shyness was somehow put aside and she ended up attracting a bit of attention: as a performer, though a somewhat low-key one.

'She didn't have much of a profile at the school,' recollected another former Northwich County pupil, who also claimed that Jennifer didn't make a great impression on many of the pupils.

'She was ordinary, really, she never stuck out in any way. And she wasn't always in all the shows – there were other people in her year who were the "acting" ones.'

The school was divided into houses – each one named after a different area in Cheshire. Jennifer was in Farndon House. And it was in a Farndon House comic sketch one afternoon during a Northwich County three-day arts festival, rather than in formal drama classes, where the 16-year-old Jennifer's talent for comic acting and improvisation surfaced.

'The house stuff was self-initiated – the staff weren't

involved in it at all. Jennifer played the part of a fortune teller and the material in the sketch had been written by the girls. And she was really, really funny. She was a year above me but I can still remember sitting there, laughing, looking at her makeup – which made her look like an old hag. She was definitely not one of the "stars" of the school as far as the general perception of her was concerned. But that day we all realised that this girl was actually really funny.

'That someone came through that Colditz place and achieved what she's done in comedy… well, it's amazing.'

Rosalind Fifield has lived in the Acton Bridge/Crowton area for most of her life and was a neighbour of the Saunders family for many years.

'My two boys went to The Grange and Jennifer's mother, Jane, taught them. She was a very good teacher,' she recalled.

'Jennifer and her family lived about two and a half miles away from us. At one point, when she was about 16, Jennifer would babysit for me and my sister Diana. Jennifer rode a lot – there's lots of riding around here. My sister and I knew her parents through the local Conservative fundraisers. They were a very nice family, very unassuming. And Jennifer was very quiet and well mannered – a good babysitter.

'But she wasn't at all outgoing. You'd never have believed that this girl would end up playing someone like Edina in *Absolutely Fabulous*.'

Rosalind's sister, Diana Mather, a former BBC TV presenter, remembered Jennifer's father Tom as 'a very witty, charming man'.

'Maybe the sense of humour comes from her father. The family were very close – and very private. That's probably given her a very good "rock" on which to build her own family life and career.'

It's often at university that talented performers or writers start to really spread their wings. Not surprisingly, given her solidly middle-class background, Jennifer's parents were keen for her to head off to university after leaving Northwich County with three A-levels. One brother won a place at Cambridge, but Jennifer didn't seem to be destined towards heading in the same direction.

Approaches were made to various universities, including an application for a course in combined sciences at Leicester. But Jennifer, while intelligent, just didn't shine in the university interview rounds. In today's language, the shy girl, who until that point had been mostly interested in horse riding, had poor presentation skills.

'It was a cause of some frustration all round,' Jennifer told the *Daily Mail* in November 1992. 'The problem was always the same. I wasn't really interested in any interview. I would sit there, apathetic and morose, not caring either way.'

'I got turned down by every university I went to interview with,' she told the *Liverpool Daily Post* in 2012. 'I sort of wish I had gone to university but your life is what happens as you live it. So much else wouldn't have happened.'

After a fairly brief period working as an au pair in Italy: 'They were horrible, rich brat English children,' she recalled to *OK Magazine* in 1996, she returned home to Cheshire to find that her mother, Jane, determined to get her daughter's further education resolved somehow, had a list of degree courses waiting for Jennifer on the kitchen table.

Jennifer opted for a BEd drama teaching course at London's Central School of Speech & Drama in Swiss Cottage, north London. Not because she had an overwhelming desire to teach, far from it.

'I thought it would be cool to go to London,' she recalled.

So the application went off and she got her interview at Central, even though she had little real experience – or knowledge – of drama itself. Writing a comic sketch with other girls was one thing. Serious theatre was another.

'I think they were desperate for people on this course. I hadn't done any plays at school. At the interview I had to lie and I said I'd seen Dostoevsky's *The Rivals* as I remembered seeing a poster at the Royal Exchange in Manchester.'

Then the interviewers asked what she thought of the play. (Little did they know that Jennifer had only ever seen one play in her entire life, and that was *Charley's Aunt*).

'Oh, very good,' she said, deadpan, not realising that Dostoevsky had not written *The Rivals* – the author of the play was Sheridan.

Perhaps her examiners saw through the bluff – this was the Central School of Speech & Drama, after all, the UK's most prestigious drama school, so they probably would have realised that Jennifer was winging it. But they were sufficiently impressed by her exam results – you needed only one A-level to get in – and her improvisation routine – with a broom – to accept Jennifer. She was in.

Many of theatre's and television's greatest names have trained at Central. Judi Dench, Sir Laurence Olivier, Vanessa

Redgrave, Lindsay Duncan, Rupert Everett and Kristin Scott Thomas all studied their craft there. So she was following in the footsteps of the great and the good.

But there was no grand plan, no ambition, no overwhelming desire to forge a career in show business or to act on the stage. The three-year drama teaching course just seemed like a good idea at the time and a chance to live in London – far more exciting to a 19-year-old girl than the prospect of quiet rural life in Cheshire. And it would turn out to be exciting. But not in any way Jennifer or anyone who knew her would ever have imagined...

The Central School of Speech & Drama is located on the border of Swiss Cottage and Belsize Park, north London, just off the traffic-clogged streets of Finchley Road and on the site of the old Embassy Theatre.

Today, it directly faces a streamlined, ultra-modern, sprawling community area complete with library, gym complex and the prestigious Hampstead Theatre. The houses in the surrounding streets are expensive and very upmarket: not much change from half a million pounds just for a small flat.

But back then, in 1977, the area itself was totally different: quite scruffy, large but very shabby and rundown nineteenth-century villas and houses alongside post-war blocks of local authority flats and concrete high rises.

Students at Central who shared the mostly grotty flats in the peeling stucco houses in the area were likely to be living with mice, ever-complaining ancient landladies, toilets on the landing and kitchens boasting a bath – with a lid on it.

The Thatcherite property renovation frenzy that took over London in the 1980s was still in the future.

And those students, like Jennifer, who were starting their drama teaching course that year, in the class called T80, were a mixed bag: mostly quite young, out to have fun above all else, all sorts of backgrounds.

The course itself was quite new. And the drama teaching students were very much seen as the 'poor relations' to the more exalted drama students on the acting course, who mostly ignored the teaching students' very existence. Boys wore tights and ballet shoes. Girls were issued with a regulation black leotard, thick black tights and a full-length practice skirt to wear in rehearsals and dance classes.

The routine at T80 was 9am to 5pm five days a week, something that Jennifer initially struggled to keep up with.

'Some days I would cycle to school, get there too late and then just ride home again. I couldn't quite get into gear for about a year,' she said of those Central days.

For the drama teaching students, there was a busy schedule. Each day consisted of classes for voice, movement, teaching of drama and poetry, and regular sessions where students learned more about stagecraft, skills such as building sets or making costumes. And, of course, there was teaching practice. And this bit came as a huge surprise to Jennifer, who, for some reason, hadn't actually taken on board the fact that the course was aimed at... training teachers of drama.

'It was a shock when I discovered I'd been put on a teaching course. It never occurred to me they'd eventually throw me into a school with real children,' she recalled.

But it was in the daily movement class, in the autumn of 1977, in the school's big training room-cum-studio with its huge mirrors and barres along the walls, when fate stepped in for Jennifer in that first year at college.

The new teaching students, all shapes and sizes, clad in the most unforgiving garment known to man – the black leotard – were reluctantly going through their paces doing warm-ups, exercises, swinging their legs, when a new 19-year-old girl stepped into the class, a couple of days late and, unlike Jennifer, desperately keen on the idea of learning how to be a drama teacher.

Enter Dawn French, nervous that she had missed the all-important first bit, the initial 'bonding' sessions that usually take place at the beginning of a study course.

In the time-honoured fashion, Jennifer and Dawn checked each other out while struggling to bend, stretch and follow the warm-up exercises. Jennifer, always swift to spot comic potential, seemed rather amused at the ridiculousness of all this 'movement' and didn't manage to hide her feelings. No grins were exchanged or serious eye contact made directly between the two girls. They didn't 'connect' instantly. Not at all. And certain assumptions were made when they chatted briefly afterwards. These assumptions proved to be totally incorrect, of course. But it definitely wasn't love at first sight.

According to Dawn French, this mutual disinterest was mostly down to her own insecurities – and their shared RAF childhoods.

'I liked the look of Jennifer. But she seemed far too confident and intimidating for me,' remembered Dawn in an interview with the *Daily Mail*.

'I arrived after term had started because my dad had just died. People had already started to get their little groups together and Jen was part of quite a confident group of posh girls and it was difficult for me to fit in.

'Both our fathers were in the RAF but Jen's dad was an officer and my dad wasn't. Jen was the epitome of the upper-middle-class girl whereas I was upper working-class. I was slightly intimidated by posh people – and I thought that officers and their children were posh people. Now I recognise that's a foolish thing. Rank delineates in the Forces and it takes you a lifetime to get over it. It ultimately doesn't matter but it was a big part of my childhood: you were constantly told where you belonged.'

To Jennifer, Dawn French was a stout, bossy person, horribly keen on being a drama teacher: 'I didn't take the course seriously and she did. I think she was the only person on the course who really wanted to be one, so that was a bit of a barrier between us.

'And she annoyed me greatly: she was very outgoing and popular, just back from a year in New York. And I was quite quiet and introverted. I was probably considered a bit laid-back – or sullen,' Jennifer told *More* magazine.

'She wore a Yale sweatshirt, baseball boots and a baseball cap at a slanty angle – all quite nauseating. We looked completely different. She thought I was snotty. I wasn't – I was really shy and quiet.

'Dawn seemed very grown-up and settled. And I felt a bit junior to her. She was very organised and I felt useless beside her.

'I think when you're at a certain age you're in a sort of vacuum, not quite a real person yet. I was very rigid and introverted. I had a very stiff lip – from flute playing, not inbreeding – and Dawn was terribly bouncy. But also in a sort of vacuum, like me.'

For the first couple of years of the teaching course, the pair remained distinctly unimpressed by each other. No real bonds of friendship or camaraderie developed. It wasn't until 1979 and the start of their third year on the course when things really changed.

One of the students in their year had a boyfriend who owned a nearby property that had recently been converted. It was up for rent – and eight people could share it. Dawn French was certainly up for the new conversion as she was fed up with sharing a tiny flat somewhat inconveniently situated in scruffy Kensal Rise. Then she heard that Jennifer Saunders was also interested.

'I was definitely under-joyed by the prospect of that,' said Dawn in her memoir *Dear Fatty*. 'It wasn't that we actively disliked each other, not at all, just that we had been on the same course and not really found each other, not really bothered, both assuming that the other wasn't our type. I thought she might be the only one in the flat I wouldn't be able to relate to.'

Yet there is nothing quite like the proximity of living under the same roof for getting to know someone quickly. Particularly since the new flat, in nearby Steele's Road, was within walking distance of the college. And not long after they had moved in, as the two students walked together down Fellows Road en route to the college in Adamson

Road, the assumptions they had made started to crumble. And there were a few surprises.

They did have things in common: Dawn too had spent time in Italy au pairing, and when they exchanged their experiences of living on RAF camps, their 'always on the move' childhoods, it turned out that they had even briefly had the same best friend, another RAF child.

'When I was 11, I had a best friend, and very good fun. Then she left and I was heartbroken. Jen and I discovered that she went to another camp and there she was Jennifer's best friend. We put out a call for her on the radio once but she never got in touch,' recalled Dawn in an interview with the *Daily Mail* in December 1993.

But there was another, much bigger discovery in those walks: the two students, one short and effervescent, bubbling over with enthusiasm, the other slightly taller, seemingly cool and languid, shared the same surreal sense of humour. They could make each other laugh like drains. All the time. Both had a similar sense of the ridiculous – and they loved to act it out. Frequently.

Dawn soon realised that behind Jennifer's rather mysterious façade was a bright, extremely attractive and intriguing person. Jennifer saw that behind Dawn's super-organised, somewhat bossy front was an outrageously funny, warm individual. Both relished taking the mickey out of everything, especially the college course, puncturing its serious 'actorly' side. At times, they would find themselves laughing consistently from the minute they walked out of the Steele's Road flat until they arrived at college.

They didn't quite realise it but, at the end of the 1970s, the two young women, laughing themselves close to tears as they walked to college, perched on bar stools and taking the mickey out of the elderly male drinkers in the nearby pubs in Chalk Farm (they've never admitted it but this was surely their early inspiration for the legendary 'Two Fat Old Men' sketch) or just lolling around in their living room, making up more and more ridiculous situations, were shaping an incredibly close-knit relationship – and, of course, an exceptional showbiz career that neither could ever have dreamed of.

How could they? For a start, female comedy duos were unknown territory. At the time, no one could envisage the idea of a female double act on TV like Morecambe & Wise. Only their parents' World War Two generation could remember the big BBC radio stars of the 1940s – Elsie and Doris Waters, or 'Gert and Daisy' as their immensely popular act was known. And while stand-up comedy was about to revolutionise the entertainment world, female stand-ups were still relatively unknown, especially on television.

Yet shared laughter, day in, day out, creates something special, unbreakable. And it stimulates sparky, creative minds. These two would always share this wonderful bond of laughter; they still have it to this day. The old saying 'two heads are better than one' springs to mind, though in this case it was more like 'two minds that can constantly spot the comic potential of nearly everything around them'.

'Once we moved in, we broke down our prejudices about each other and realised we had a similarly bizarre sense of humour,' Jennifer recalled in an interview with the *Daily Mail* in June 2000.

'Dawn made me laugh so much. We used to play the cruellest practical jokes on everybody in the flat. They were very juvenile. We used to hide in the laundry basket and pop out. Or try to make severed head things out of a cabbage and bang them on windows. We shared the flat with people who worked for a living. It was tragic – and it became my career. The joy of our relationship is you never quite grow up.'

Such was the hilarity of those times sharing the Steele's Road flat that their experiences would eventually inspire the riotous 1985 ITV series *Girls on Top*, penned by Jennifer, Dawn and Ruby Wax. The location of the fictional flat was changed from north-west London to Chelsea, but there was a wealth of fantastic comic material from those flat-sharing Central days to draw on.

Like chaotic young sharers almost everywhere, living with five or six other people meant a 'cleaning' rota that never functioned (other than as a precursor to rows), an abundance of extremely stale food in a messy kitchen, frequently consumed at strange hours – and, of course, party after party.

Dawn and Jennifer would sit in the front room at Steele's Road, inventing over-the-top characters, messing around and generally creating mayhem, performing in the house for the benefit of some of their more tolerant flatmates.

Jennifer, whose bedroom was right at the top of the house, was known to have really untidy quarters. At one point, the flat was broken into.

'The police said: "Well, it is quite bad but the worst is that room at the top." And, of course, nobody had been in there,' recalled Dawn. 'She used to be up to her knees in old pants.'

Childish as it may sound now, the girls would enjoy dressing up, punk style. Sometimes they'd wear chamber pots on their heads, accompanied by long black plastic macs. Then they'd go out on the street or jump onto the Tube to see if people were frightened of their somewhat bizarre appearance.

'We'd hang tampons on our ears and have safety pins stuck in various places. It was a perfect time to have no money – you could go to Swiss Cottage market, pick up great clothes and just wear them.' Jennifer told *The Sunday Times* in November 1993.

The duo would often go to other people's parties clad in these outrageous outfits; they got to like doing it so much, they dressed up like this all the time.

'Then we made up a punk song to perform at someone's party. I knew about three chords on the guitar; Dawn knew about two. We called ourselves the Menopatzi [translation: less mad] Sisters. And the song was a little number about a gerbil,' Jennifer recalled.

The Menopatzi Sisters, the girls decided, were middle-aged performers in black leotards and red Latex swimming hats, who were the last in a long line of an Italian circus family: they were a circus mime act. They were also useless.

In the girls' last year at Central, in an end-of-term cabaret act – after some initial hesitation but egged on by their friends – they performed two comic sketches they had written for the other students: the Menopatzi Sisters and another sketch called 'Psychodrama', involving two American women who were obsessed with their spiritual well-being.

'It was at the time when anything "alternative" was coming in, things like people having therapy. Even the word "muesli" was funny. It was a kind of therapy/muesli-based act,' said Jennifer.

The humour in their sketches didn't come from telling a series of jokes. It was more in the girls' performance and character study. And their cabaret act went down really well. People laughed a lot. Both girls went to bed that night knowing the evening had been a success. They could make other people laugh, not just each other. Yet neither had any intention, at that stage, of developing their act into some sort of career.

'I remember thinking how easy it was. We seemed to pick up on each other's humour and absolutely clicked,' recalled Jennifer.

By 1980, the girls had graduated and gone off in different directions: Dawn to teach drama at Parliament Hill School for Girls, a comprehensive in north London, her long-held ambition now reaching fulfilment. Jennifer moved to a shared flat in a shabby house in far-off (and posh) Chelsea. There was the odd menial job occasionally. But teaching, she had already decided at Central, definitely wasn't going to play any part in her future. She had had a taste of it as a student – and she was adamant that it wasn't right for her.

'I had no enthusiasm for teaching. I'd spent some time

in an Ursuline convent in Wimbledon and then taught for 10 weeks at a high school in Peckham. I was popular. But no good,' she told *Woman's Own* magazine in February 1993.

'I could never see it being my career just because I liked the kids. I couldn't take the staffroom politics.'

'I thought that when Dawn and I left college that would be the end of the relationship,' said Jennifer in an interview with the *Daily Mail* in June 2000. 'And I was quite content to be on the dole. I did nothing for months on end. I was never desperately ambitious. I had a feeling that something might float along eventually, whereas Dawn has a capacity for work I just don't have.'

Yet whatever their feelings after graduation, the two girls did take something very important away with them from their time at Central, a crucial factor in the life of any successful actor or performer: the 'P' word – professionalism.

'You were taught to be professional and respect others. Central took the prima donna out of you,' remembered one former graduate of the Central drama teaching course in the late 1970s. 'Professionalism was the overriding thing you took from the course; you did the very best you could. And you can see that in Jennifer Saunders and Dawn French – it's all about being equal.'

Time passed. Dawn was enjoying her new life, discovering the many challenges involved in teaching, relishing the chance to connect with inner-city kids, whose lives could only benefit from learning more about drama.

Jennifer, however, spent most of her day doing *The Times* crossword, drinking coffee and generally having a laid-back existence. Plan? Career? Who needed those things? Wasn't it enough to be young and carefree?

She has freely admitted that she had no plans or goals whatsoever. In an interview with *The New York Times* in July 1995, she said: 'I was just sitting about and getting the dole, if I could be bothered. We went off the dole because we were never up in time. We used to live on these mattresses and there was actually a path worn in the dust on the carpet from our bed to the door.'

But their lives were about to change permanently. And the instrument of change was a small theatre located inside a Soho strip joint, right in the heart of London's West End, in an area full of porno cinemas and sex shops selling hard-core magazines, an insalubrious backdrop for the launch of a group of hugely talented male comic performers – whose fates would be very closely intertwined with those of the two ex-Central graduates.

And it was Jennifer, lounging around in her flat one day, flicking through a paper, who started it all.

'I saw an advert in *The Stage* [the entertainment industry trade paper] looking for new acts to perform at a comedy/cabaret venue called The Comic Strip in Soho.

'I remember thinking: "I wonder if Dawn would be interested." I don't think anybody else would have touched me with a bargepole, but it just seemed totally natural to do it with Dawn.'

A phone call to an enthusiastic Dawn resulted in the pair heading off to their first ever audition at the Comic Strip's home, the 200-seater Boulevard Theatre above the Raymond Revue Bar in Walker's Court. (The Raymond

Revue Bar was a popular Soho strip joint owned by Paul Raymond, the celebrated club owner and entrepreneur.) Undaunted by the louche surroundings, once up in the theatre the pair waited their turn, watching a man on stage juggling lobster pots.

Then they were on, performing their old college sketch about the neurotic Americans. And, amazingly, they got in!

'We weren't very good,' said Jennifer. 'But they were desperate for women, to make it more politically correct, and we were the first living beings with boobs to come through the door.

'I don't know why it didn't seem strange, working above a strip club, but it didn't.

'We got hired for the bum nights, which were Tuesday and Wednesday, when there were few people in the theatre. Sometimes we outnumbered the audience.

'Such blind, blind panic. We just used to make anything up, silly stuff that made us laugh. I used to look through the crack in the door, praying nobody would be there.'

Arnold Brown is a Scottish comedian who was working as a stand-up comic at The Comic Strip at that time. He witnessed the girls' memorable first audition.

'Their parody of American tourists in London was clever. It was funny, but it didn't give any hint of how wonderful they were going to be in the future. It wasn't a sensational sketch, but it was well written, very skillful.'

Brown's immediate enthusiasm for the girls' double act led to him encouraging them to listen to tapes of the female double act of yesteryear, Gert and Daisy. Today, he remembers the youthful Jennifer as 'quite an English rose, very good-looking, good bone structure. And there was obviously something special between the two girls that really connected.

'They fitted into The Comic Strip perfectly; the boys at The Comic Strip were over the top, a very testosterone line-up. I fitted into it because I was a laid-back contrast to the boys. And they fitted in because it was nice to see two girls doing their stuff.'

Today, we take female comic performers for granted, yet in 1980 they were a novelty: performers on the newly emerging cabaret/stand-up circuit were almost exclusively male. And overtly political stand-up comedy itself was relatively new too, though the arrival of a Tory government and Margaret Thatcher in 1979 was starting to be a strong focus for comedy. Although female performers such as Jenny Lecoat and Jenny Eclair (who went on to a successful career as a comedy writer) were poised to launch careers in the new comedy/cabaret circuit in the early 1980s, their early work involved a more 'punk' sensibility than Jennifer and Dawn, whose sketch-based comedy was essentially two women engaged in chatty dialogue, without any heavy emphasis on political issues or feminism and the war between the sexes.

This difference proved to be helpful, too. 'There were a lot of pro-feminist hard-hitting acts about. But we didn't do that, which was to our advantage,' recalled Jennifer.

You can be at the right place at the right time, yet burgeoning creativity needs to be free-flowing and without limits. Because they had hardly any external direction and total freedom to experiment with their material and shape their sketches however they chose, the era was a wonderfully free outlet for their talents. Before long, they were on stage, performing their sketches, several nights a week.

Jennifer has always had great affection for those early attempts at comedy.

'I loved those days. No responsibilities. We went where we liked, stayed out as long as we wanted and if the audience didn't laugh, we didn't care. London itself just felt great – you had nothing to care about, no property, nothing. We didn't think of it as a job, it was just a bit of fun.'

The pair earned £5 each for an evening's work. The act was quite basic: sometimes they would just find a prop and work around that, find something to do with it.

'We had one sketch where we dressed like *Thunderbirds* puppets and one of us said: "What's the time, Brains?" The other said: "Six o'clock, Mr Tracy." That was it. God knows how anyone thought it was funny.'

And so in this small theatre with its lingering haze of stale cigarette smoke, audiences who were often drunk – or had drifted in from outside as an antidote to being hassled on the street by overeager sex touts – the two women launched their careers in comedy.

It was bottom-of-the-ladder, hit-and-miss stuff, still a tad daunting for an essentially shy person like Jennifer, who had only started to overcome her performer's nerves during her time at Central, but it was a real beginning, an incredibly lucky break to be caught up in performing in something as radically new as The Comic Strip – which eventually proved to be unique in the history of British comedy. Their talents definitely didn't develop overnight, but they couldn't have found a better place to launch them.

Dawn continued to teach by day, heading for the bright lights of Soho by night, enjoying the contrast between the two very different worlds while fervently hoping that no one from her school would rumble her other life.

Initially, they tried to create a new sketch each night – until it dawned on them that the audience changed every night anyway so they had more time to produce different material, sometimes working on the scripts at Dawn's studio in the school after hours.

'We didn't know anything about it really. Because we thought you had to change your costumes and material every night at first, by Saturday it got pretty bad,' Jennifer remembered.

Yet soon, as the girls began to also perform at The Comedy Store, another Soho strip joint hosting a popular late-night comedy venue that had started to attract a great deal of attention even before The Comic Strip's launch as a venue, their shows in the two Soho venues, just a short walk apart from each other, kick-started a series of events that would transform everything.

The Comedy Store, located in the Gargoyle Club in Soho's Dean Street (and modelled on the successful, similarly named Comedy Store in Los Angeles), was a venue where new stand-up comedy acts performed each night. It had also been drawing the West End crowds, mostly thanks to the talents of a group of anarchic male comic performers, all young and very much poised to take Brit comedy by storm.

At one point, not long before Jennifer and Dawn got their break at The Comic Strip, this male group had 'defected' from The Comedy Store and taken their talents to The Comic Strip, the brainchild of their unofficial gang leader Peter Richardson and a rival venue for their new type of anarchic, character-based comedy performance.

In fact, both venues would eventually go down in comedy history as the birthplace of what came to be called 'alternative comedy': young, hip, aggressive, rude, sometimes political stand-up that eschewed the more traditional form of comedy, i.e. telling jokes, and came to be the comic motif of the times. It was usually angry, sometimes ranting, but it was also very, very funny.

The names of these comic actors are essentially a roll call of Brit TV's late twentieth-century laughtermeisters: driven by the talents of The Comic Strip's founder, Peter Richardson – with star turn Alexei Sayle acting as compère or MC – the core Comic Strip performers were Ade Edmondson and Rik Mayall (who had formed a double act, 20th Century Coyote, during their days together at Manchester University) and Nigel Planer (one half of another double act with Peter Richardson called The Outer Limits), with occasional guest turns from performers such as Ben Elton, Keith Allen, Chris Langham and Robbie Coltrane.

This was a comic potpourri like no other: a revolutionary group dubbed 'alternative comedians' at the time, but essentially the fast-rising generation of TV comic entertainers of the 1980s, riding a new wave of anarchic comedy that was about to sweep the country, first on stage and then on television. And Jennifer and Dawn were now working alongside them. Regularly.

Initially, it was all a bit intimidating.

Jennifer recalled: 'We were in awe of the boys at first, because they'd been at it six months ahead of us. Dawn and I shared a little dressing room. The boys were next door in a horrible sweaty room. They performed in a hot theatre, night after night, and they never cleaned their suits. It was fairly evil in there, but it was like being part of a family, growing up together.

'The boys would never tell us what to do; they didn't give us hints. But just by looking at them, we picked up an idea of what we might be aiming towards.'

Essentially, the girls' relationship with the boys was like having a large group of older brothers, lots of teasing and joshing – they would all have to go through the strip club each night to reach their dressing rooms.

It was distinctly edgy and fun – the strip club audiences, mostly ageing businessmen, watched the strip shows in another theatre, but they would sometimes have to rub shoulders at The Comic Strip with the younger, fashionable, alternative comedy audience in their trendy New Romantic gear simply because there was only one bar.

Despite their relative inexperience, Jennifer and Dawn held their own, writing and experimenting with new material. Sometimes they got the laughs and cheers, at other times they would fall flat. Encouraged by the good nights, they soon learned to tough out the bad.

'Rik and Ade had a very aggressive stage act so they could punch their way through any negative feedback from the audience,' recollected Jennifer, 'but we'd be the first act and weren't right in the audience's faces. So the crowd had plenty of opportunities to shout "Get off! Get off!" We were complete novices. We'd come straight from college and had never done anything like this before.'

They were on a real learning curve. And they still, for the life of them, couldn't come up with the right name for their double act.

They had spent ages trying to think of something amusing. Names like Kitch 'n' Tiles were debated. And discarded. Until one night, Alexei Sayle, fed up with their indecision, took the initiative in typical style. 'Please welcome French and Saunders,' he told the audience. And that was it.

At The Comedy Store, the atmosphere was much more frenetic than at The Comic Strip. It was a bit of a bear pit. There was a gong and the general idea was that performers could stay on stage for a short period before being 'gonged' off. Sometimes the noisy, boisterous crowd wanted people gonged off straight away. It was confrontational, competitive and very much a male environment. Someone would shout out a racist remark and fights would break out.

'We were like the early days of motoring: a crazy ride,' is how Alexei Sayle described it.

At the girls' first night at The Comedy Store, the act before them was interrupted by a racist heckler. Bottles and chairs flew; total mayhem. The police even turned up to deal with the miscreant. On another occasion a group of boozy men on a stag night yelled out to the girls: 'Show us your tits!' At which point, Dawn, in teacher fashion, walked to the edge of the stage and ordered the yobs to shut up and be quiet. It worked. As for the gong, the girls soon discovered that even if they got gonged off quite quickly, they still got paid.

Don Ward, co-founder of The Comedy Store, viewed them very much as comedy actresses rather than stand-up comediennes.

'There was no star quality about them at all. They might last five minutes or they might even get to eight minutes, but sooner or later the audience would have them off. They didn't seem to give a damn. They'd shrug their shoulders, pick up their money and say: "Right, Don, see you next week."

'And off they'd go.'

Although the girls were gradually being absorbed into The Comic Strip/Richardson ensemble, which was essentially three double acts: the girls, Ade and Rik, and Nigel and Peter, with Alexei Sayle as the MC, they continued to perform in both. Such was the buzz around The Comedy Store that big names started dropping in to watch the acts. Robin Williams leapt up onto the stage to everyone's delight one night. Bianca Jagger was spotted in the audience. And Jack Nicholson turned up to look – and laugh. Yet equally, the Comic Strip was drawing the attention of influential people in the entertainment world.

As former Head of BBC Entertainment, Paul Jackson recalled: 'In a way, The Comic Strip became the new punk because there was an anger. Keith Allen once threw beer over an *Evening Standard* critic.'

Then, at the end of the summer of 1981, Peter Richardson's Comic Strip group were offered their breakthrough gig: a national tour around the UK. This was scheduled to be followed by a tour of Australia, with a stint at the prestigious Adelaide Festival in South Australia in March 1982. It was decision time: should Dawn ditch her safe teaching career in north London for a chance to expand both girls' horizons as comic performers?

Dawn felt torn. She deliberated until her boss at the school pointed out that, much as they didn't want to lose her, the chance to go on tour to Australia was a once-in-a-lifetime opportunity. When a real chance beckons, you recognise it, and grab it with both hands. And anyway, Jennifer and Dawn were having a really good time.

You only have to watch clips of those far-off days in Soho to see just how much fun they were having: Jennifer as the neurotic American Diana (complete with 1980s hairdo and shiny white top) while her friend from back home, Muriel (Dawn sporting an equally odd 1980s streaky mullet hairdo), pops up from the audience to share her delight at meeting another American – and going to the 'Towerr of Lundin – and all the little beef burgers there'. It's not that funny, not by the standards of what came afterwards, but with those two nervy tourists, you can spot the genesis, the beginnings of the satirical comic style that was to propel them towards popularity.

'We decided to have a go. If it was awful, we had each other. And we'd buy a bottle of Blue Nun and go home,' recalled Jennifer.

But from that point on, from when The Comic Strip tour

started out, cheap plonk like Blue Nun (a big favourite of the late 1970s) was on its way out. Within a few years they would be quaffing Bolly, sweetie – from the finest crystal glasses, of course.

CHAPTER 2

THE COMIC
STRIP YEARS

During the summer of 1981, The Comic Strip gang went on the road on their first ever tour, travelling across the UK in a big bus, performing nightly in different venues, which were often small – and occasionally sleazy. Fringe comedy/cabaret venues were gradually popping up all over the place, thanks to the increasing popularity of late-night stand-up and live cabaret, but some of those venues were quite tatty.

'Our opening night was in a porn cinema in the centre of Glasgow,' recalled Alexei Sayle. 'Peter Richardson could get a bit experimental with venues sometimes, but we were heartbreakingly young and optimistic.'

'We were terrified to come to Scotland because we'd heard all the stories – the place was well known as being a graveyard for comics,' added Dawn. 'I thought we're more gentle, we don't go for the jugular. So they're going to kill us.'

In fact, the Glasgow reception was quite warm. 'I nearly cried on stage – the welcome was fantastic.'

The digs were cheap and often grotty – cigarette burns on the duvet, cracked sinks, tepid water to wash in. Occasionally they would check in only to find someone still asleep in their room.

'If we were lucky enough to have a room with a shower, usually it turned out to be in the same room,' said Jennifer. 'We couldn't afford to pay for a separate bathroom.'

Arnold Brown also went on that Comic Strip tour as part of the ensemble. 'We went all over the provinces, to Nottingham, the Oxford Playhouse, sometimes working in nightclubs. We were one of the first comedy groups to go out on the road at the time and the crowds were very enthusiastic because it was so new. I even took my girlfriend of the time, Liz, with me on the tour.'

The Comic Strip's sketches, on stage, were sometimes performed in less than desirable circumstances: at one venue, the electricity supply was so limited, it was a toss-up between the sound and the lights. But while they could continue to use some of the material they'd used in the Soho venues for the UK tour, Jennifer and Dawn knew that with the Australian tour ahead of them, they would have to start writing new material, create more new sketches for their double act.

Going out on the road, improvising their scripts as they moved around, was the point where they really started to develop their own style. And the attention and publicity

The Comic Strip group was getting was incremental, as is often the case.

Each tiny step forward seemed like a big deal. There was a live comedy album called *The Comic Strip*, released in September 1981 by Springtime Records, on which Jennifer and Dawn performed their seven-minute American 'Psychodrama' sketch.

'When we recorded the show and made an album – which sold about six copies – that seemed like a really big thing,' said Jennifer. 'Then being on the radio seemed like another biggie. But the biggest thing ever for Dawn and me was when we actually got our names listed in *Time Out*.' Before, it usually said: 'Alexei Sayle and guests'. But this time it was French and Saunders.

The Comic Strip tour of Australia in March 1982 was a fantastic gig for the newcomers. What was not to like? Big blue skies, wide-open spaces, swimming pools, endless golden beaches and a fresh environment. And although as performers at the Adelaide Festival – essentially an arts festival with the emphasis on culture with a capital 'C' – they didn't make much impact, they relished the chance to be involved in such a major event – Australia's equivalent of the Edinburgh Festival. With endless sunshine.

Jim Sharman, the theatre director who directed the original *Rocky Horror Show* and the movie of the musical in the 1970s, was the Artistic Director of the Adelaide Festival at the time.

'When I invited English comedians from The Comic Strip to the festival they were thought a curious and slightly tasteless choice – and they passed without much attention,' he recalled. 'Today, having made *French and Saunders* and *Ab Fab*, no doubt they would be more culturally acceptable.'

Perhaps Sharman was criticising the cultural snobbishness of the Adelaide arts scene, rather than the performances themselves. Dawn French, in *Dear Fatty*, recollected the somewhat obvious contrast between The Comic Strip group's youthful Brit exuberance – splashing around in their hotel swimming pool, larking about generally – and the more refined elegance of some of the other festival performers.

'I remember that the Pina Bausch dance troupe were also staying there and were relaxing on their loungers, watching us scream about. There they were, all lithe and brown and elegant and slinkily nonchalant. There we were, all overexcited and goofy and fat and white. And so, so British.'

Enjoyable as it was, the Australian tour had mixed results. The local press believed that the group were not sufficiently alternative to merit the title. The catch-all tag 'alternative comedy' was frequently being used by the British press to describe all new comedy acts and The Comic Strip group disliked the name.

Alternative comedy was, in the main, quite political and left wing, sometimes espousing hard-line feminism and attacking authority head on. So the right-on, mostly left-leaning Aussie writers probably expected something along those lines from the Brits, rather than the character-driven, if sometimes confrontational work of The Comic Strip team. One Sydney gig in a big university campus theatre fell flat: no publicity, small audiences. Another booking in Melbourne produced similar results. But nothing on earth could dent the gang's excitement and enthusiasm. They flew home with big hopes for the future.

If anything, the Australian tour cemented Jennifer and Dawn's relationship with the group. And, even more importantly, there were already huge breakthroughs into TV in the wind: two months before the Aussie tour, Ade and Rik had collaborated with Ben Elton (who had been at Manchester University with them) and Rik's then girlfriend, Lise Mayer, to create a pilot show for BBC2 called *The Young Ones*.

Around the same time, Peter Richardson had taken some of his ideas for Comic Strip comedy films to Jeremy Isaacs, then the boss of the new Channel 4 – which had not yet been launched.

Thanks to the rivalry of TV broadcasters – the BBC were initially reluctant to consider *The Young Ones*, with its totally hysterical comic anarchy and complicated special effects for the time – everything now started to shift in the girls' favour, as their impact slowly grew as the only female double act of its kind.

Jennifer and Dawn's strong, challenging brand of humour, sending up the pretentious and using each other's personalities as a basis for their sketches, was seen by TV producers as just as daring as the boys' somewhat more outrageous work.

So when the BBC discovered that Channel 4 were considering using the other Comic Strip talents, post-launch, in films, they were worried they might lose everyone in The Comic Strip to their new competitor. And they quickly gave the green light for the boys' *Young Ones* pilot. Channel 4 then commissioned the first ever run of *The Comic Strip Presents*, a series of comedy films that started filming that summer of 1982.

'We were on the front page of *Time Out* and stuff so we were the kind of place they [Channel 4] were looking for,' recalled Peter Richardson of The Comic Strip's TV breakthrough.

'I said: "We've got a very funny group of comedy actors and we could do different stories each week" – self-contained stories, films really. I was interested in making comedy films. They said: "Here's the money, make something for us." And they put it out on opening night.'

That winter's night, on 2 November 1982 at 5pm, nearly 5 million people switched on their TV sets in eager anticipation. A brand-new British TV channel was being launched with much fanfare: Channel 4, the new terrestrial broadcaster, was hoping to strike exactly the right balance between the public-service broadcasting of the BBC and the outright commercialism of ITV.

It was a nail-biter for everyone involved in the launch. Would their programming be good enough to attract viewers in the millions? And, most importantly, would it be sufficiently entertaining to draw in the Holy Grail of all sought-after audiences everywhere: the younger viewers?

Today, the first ever Channel 4 programme, *Countdown*, seems light years away in broadcasting terms from today's slick, fragmented, multi-channel, multimedia world of viewing on demand. We can poke fun at those old shows now: they seem so corny and unsophisticated.

Yet the launch of Channel 4 was important: it marked a watershed in UK television broadcasting. And, equally, it was a watershed for the relatively unknown 24-year-old Jennifer Saunders. Because Channel 4's first ever comedy show, screened at 10.30pm that first night, was the first episode of *The Comic Strip Presents*, a series of five half-hour television films made especially for TV by Peter Richardson and written and performed by Jennifer, Dawn and various members of The Comic Strip group.

Two years on from their first appearance on stage in Soho, Jennifer and Dawn were on the telly.

'It was incredible luck – all gloriously accidental,' said Jennifer.

The first Comic Strip film, *Five Go Mad in Dorset*, was a send-up of a well-loved children's book written by Enid Blyton. Or, as the Channel 4 promo put it: 'Those famous brats have a ripping time on their hols in this hilarious spoof from The Comic Strip team.'

Some 3.4 million viewers tuned in to the first Comic Strip film. Each show was heralded by its distinctive roll of drums and a bomb labelled 'Have A Nice Day' hurtling towards the map.

Certainly, some viewers thought it was fresh and unpredictable – in complete contrast to the somewhat worn-out TV comedy of the past with the traditional puns, punchline gags and double entendres. But some viewers didn't think the day was at all nice.

Five Go Mad was totally new for television, a showcase

for Channel 4's daring, upfront image, a parody of a traditional adventure stereotype, starring Julian, the leader (Peter Richardson), Dick, the somewhat earnest introvert (Adrian Edmondson), George (Dawn, playing a girl who wants to be a boy), and sweet, girly Anne (Jennifer) – and, of course, Timmy the dog, the fifth character – all on their holidays on bikes, drinking ginger beer, having slap-up meals and getting mixed up with an assortment of villains, kidnappers, scientists and other odd types.

There's an iconic black-and-white photograph of Richardson, Saunders, Edmondson and French with their bikes, smiling to camera. They do look amazingly fresh-faced and innocent, typical Enid Blyton types. That was the whole point, really, because *Five Go Mad*'s anarchic spoof went in the opposite direction from the childish, safe world of Blyton's stories – and some people thought it went too far.

Five Go Mad drew angry complaints and phone calls from viewers the following day. The idea of taking on a Great British icon like the author of so many much-loved children's books seemed shocking to some people at the time (although the broadcaster had obtained permission from Blyton's estate before going on air) and it was extremely irreverent. Lots of swearing and homosexual references. *Five Go Mad* also suggested canine cunnilingus, possibly a first for British TV. Outrageous.

Such was the volume of the complaints that The Comic Strip team got called in for meetings with the Channel 4 bosses. But the tickings-off didn't halt the proceedings. Four other Comic Strip films, all with different themes, were screened on Channel 4 in January 1983, to be followed by another series in the winter of 1983/84.

Many of the films were written by Peter Richardson and his co-writer Pete Richens. But everyone in The Comic Strip group got involved in writing at some point – it was very much a repertory company-type approach to making films. (The members of the group were all paid exactly the same amount of money.) Some of the films were written by the team of Mayall and Edmondson, and *Slags*, a send-up of sci-fi movies (with the evil Slags pitched against the nice Hawaiians), was written by Jennifer. (*Slags* was shown on Channel 4 in February 1984.)

No single member of the team took centre stage. Because The Comic Strip troupe had toured together in the UK and Australia before making the films, they had bonded creatively, knew each other well and understood how important this group collaboration would be for the end result. Which was a huge advantage.

'Having two years to work together as an ensemble before that first TV film was very useful,' recalled Jennifer. 'We had the same sensibility.'

Twelve *Comic Strip Presents* films were made between 1982 and 1984; the series continued to run on Channel 4 until 1988. Then it moved to the BBC from 1990 to 1993. And it is still going. Today, *The Comic Strip Presents* archive boasts over 40 productions, five series, ten specials and two feature films. The most recent film, *The Hunt for Tony Blair*, was screened on Channel 4 in October 2011 with Jennifer playing Margaret Thatcher (channelling an outrageous Bette Davis in *What Ever Happened to Baby Jane?*).

41

The quality of the Comic Strip films is not consistent – not all the films were well received over the years – but even now, all these years on, they are considered by comedy aficionados to have been highly influential as a breakthrough movement in comedy itself.

'It started off as anarchic, anti-establishment, and today The Comic Strip group are all establishment in one way or another,' said Kim Kinnie, TV producer and former Comedy Store participant.

'That kind of change in comedy hasn't taken place since then. And they all came in because they wanted to do comedy, play the clubs. Whereas an awful lot of kids now want to do comedy just to get on TV.'

Those early years making the Comic Strip films will always be remembered by Jennifer with fond nostalgia: 'Half the men wanted to play rock stars, the other half Clint Eastwood. Sometimes the films looked like an art film, sometimes a sitcom. There was a lot of diversity.'

Over time, actors such as Miranda Richardson, Kathy Burke, Anthony Head and Doon Mackichan all took roles in *The Comic Strip Presents* movies.

'I was always in awe of the proper actors who came into it because they would concentrate and learn their lines. I'd be thinking: "What's for lunch?"' Jennifer revealed.

Filming those early Comic Strip movies and working on location, often in Devon where Peter Richardson's family had a home, was, for Jennifer, 'the happiest, happiest time. We would film ridiculous hours: finish at two in the morning, then back filming at 6am. But you were young and you didn't mind – it was a great learning curve. With

The Comic Strip, you got to learn how it was made. You were hanging around with the director and sitting in on script meetings. Sometimes Peter could be a hard taskmaster because he writes in a particular way, but there was always scope to put in other jokes.'

For Jennifer, during this time she was also able to really explore the role of the director: 'It was so free because you learned almost everything about the direction: you could even help direct certain scenes, learn how film works, how to work with the film crew, and everything you had a suggestion for was taken, and you could go and look at the editing and help the editor; so you had control all the way along the line, which in a lot of companies you don't get.

'We'd sleep in Peter's mum's farmhouse in Devon. Or share bunk beds in cottages. It was a real collaboration, a family feeling; there was a great sense of that. Often they were weirder roles, rather than comic roles. Like I said, I was more interested in the catering. Free food! And there wasn't a sense back then that you had to fit in with what a committee of executives wanted: you were creatively left to your own devices.'

It's an ideal creative combination: learning the business first hand and, at the same time, having a good time with friends.

'We were constantly having to snog the other members of the cast, which was delightful,' recalled Jennifer. 'I think Dawn got in more snogging than me – she always had the raunchier parts. A lot of Peter's women were larger than life, lots of red lipstick. When he mimed the woman he wanted you to play, it was all hand on hip and applying lipstick.'

The Comic Strip films were shot at different times with big gaps in between them. Usually, they took about two weeks to shoot and another six to eight weeks pre-production work. Throughout 1983, Jennifer and Dawn continued to work onstage, still touring small gigs and fringe theatre venues, performing their character-linked sketches. Firm dates for the Comic Strip films were always last minute, so it was sometimes a case of trying to juggle commitments.

And because everyone in the group was busy with other things for much of the time, those gaps in *The Comic Strip Presents* proceedings meant that, when they did get together again, it tended to be full-on party time.

'We wouldn't do anything for a year,' recalled Robbie Coltrane. 'Then we'd all come together again and it was like a family reunion, on location in some hotel, catching up and getting pissed for a week.'

By November 1982, the first ever series of *The Young Ones* had gone out, too: on BBC2, just a week after the screening of *Five Go Mad in Dorset* on Channel 4. Despite its subsequent cult following, it wasn't an overnight sensation, though the anarchy of the show was established right from the word go, with frequent interruptions of the scenario – a group of psychotic students sharing a shambolic home – by wildly hilarious special effects sequences that took the whole thing right off into the stratosphere.

Viewing figures for the first series were not especially good. Around 2.5 million viewers tuned in. And it wasn't until the fifth programme had aired that the show was even reviewed by the newspapers, such was its shock value: older critics were horrified at the violence and angry dialogue.

But the show proved to be a revolutionary moment in British television: very soon the quartet of Vyvyan, the angry, 'smash everything', gormless punk (Adrian Edmondson), Rick, the right-on sociology student and Cliff Richard fan (Rik Mayall), Neil, the melancholic, laid-back, lentil-eating hippie (Nigel Planer) and the relatively normal Mike (Christopher Ryan), accompanied by Alexei Sayle as their Russian landlord, Jerzy, were being recognised as 'those blokes off the telly' around the West End clubs.

The Young Ones wasn't an enormous commercial success, but its punk sensibility had a huge cultural impact on younger people. In its own way, it was a mini revolution in British comedy. After the second series went out in 1984, the double act of Ade and Rik moved on to other, similar TV comedy series such as *Filthy, Rich & Catflap* (1987) and *Bottom* (1991–95).

Yet when it came to achieving greater recognition, the girls from The Comic Strip weren't likely to be lagging too far behind the boys. In July 1983, Jennifer and Dawn made their TV debut as a double act when they recorded a segment in a new series called *The Entertainers*, made at London Weekend Television studios for Channel 4.

The idea of the show was to introduce new acts: other performers such as Helen Lederer and Ben Elton were also showcased in the series. The pair used character sketches they had previously used to tour fringe theatre venues such as The King's Head in fashionable Islington, north London.

By now, their sketches sometimes accentuated their real-life relationship as friends, using Jennifer as the star and Dawn as the sidekick.

The duo performed their American 'Psychodrama' sketch on *The Entertainers*. However, when the show went out on Channel 4 on 6 October 1983 it was in the late slot – around 11.15pm – so hardly anyone saw it. Why? One word: clitoris. The girls had used the word in their sketch and so the nervous TV executives banished it to the late, late slot. That's how it was back then.

There were other TV gigs as comic performers: weekly slots on the irreverent, hip, 90-minute live music show *The Tube*, which ran on Channel 4 for five years from 1982, showcasing rising bands including INXS, The Police and Culture Club. Following one such slot in 1984, there were raised eyebrows – and headlines – when Dawn was the first person on British television to utter the word 'blowjob'.

Jennifer and Dawn also made brief appearances in two episodes of the BBC's *The Young Ones*: in 1982, Jennifer played Sue, Rik Mayall's girlfriend (in a hilarious and memorable scene where the unwitting Rik pulls out a Tampax from her bag), and she appeared as Helen Mucus in a 1984 episode called 'Time'.

Jennifer and Dawn also made brief cameo appearances in *The Lenny Henry Show* in 1984. And throughout this early period of their career, the pair were constantly trying out different ideas, different types of comedy writing. The results were not always to their liking.

At one point, they started to write a TV play.

'It was pathetic,' recalled Jennifer, 'we covered it in rather tragic little comments in brackets: "not a big laugh here, more of a wry smile".'

But as their TV careers built up, personal relationships were starting to take centre stage in their lives.

Dawn had briefly met Lenny Henry in 1981 during the live Comic Strip performances: he had come backstage to meet the pair after the show. Already successful at the time, at just 23, he didn't make much of an impact on Dawn.

But in 1982, while Alexei Sayle was filming an episode of a six-part TV show in London called *Whoops Apocalypse*, Dawn and Lenny met, by sheer chance, in the queue to go into the studio, joining the live audience to watch their friend Alexei. And that's when they clicked: the beginning of a decades-long, loving relationship between two of Britain's funniest, most versatile performers. From that point on, they soon became an item, though for many months they kept quiet about it to the wider world.

Yet Dawn, having fallen madly in love with Lenny very quickly, has since owned up to her massive insecurity with men when Jennifer was around.

'I was always scared blokes would like Jennifer more than me. Which they always did. Blokes would chat me up and I'd think: "I'm going to get a snog here." And then they'd say: "Where's Jennifer?"

'When I first met Lenny I thought I must keep him away from Jennifer or he'll go for her instead. It's a natural reaction. If you love someone you expect they'll love the same people as you.'

Jennifer also remembered that illogical insecurity. She had unwittingly turned up at Dawn's front door for a writing session that Dawn had totally forgotten about after her first encounter with Lenny.

'She acted like a madwoman when she met Lenny. She wouldn't let me into her house the day after she slept with him because of her paranoia about him fancying me,' she recalled.

Dawn French and Lenny Henry were married at St Paul's Church in London's Covent Garden in October 1984. The reception was at The Savoy Hotel. Jennifer, of course, was over the moon about her friend's happiness. However, it wouldn't be too long before she too would be making those same vows at the altar – curiously enough, with some considerable assistance from Dawn...

Adrian Edmondson and Jennifer Saunders come from similar backgrounds: middle-class Forces kids who got involved with a group of other talented actors, writers and performers as young acting graduates at a very early stage in their career. In one way, you could say that it was inevitable, given the close working relationships of The Comic Strip ensemble, that something might happen between them: after all, brief, intense relationships are a hallmark of show business; very attractive people thrown closely together for short periods of time while away on tour or working on location. Sometimes the relationships end when the shoot or gig finishes, but occasionally they are the start of something much bigger.

For these two, it was very much a slow, slow burn over a five-year period. They liked each other, they laughed together all the time at their anarchic creations or ideas – and they always had a fantastic time collaborating on location for Richardson's Comic Strip movies. But although their paths crossed regularly for work and they knew each other extremely well, the relationship remained determinedly platonic. Even when they weren't working, they would sometimes spend time together. But that was it.

'We're both into cars and Jennifer had an Alfa Romeo Spider and I had an old Mark 10 Jaguar and we'd drive round Britain together,' recalled Ade. 'We went out platonically for ages – and slowly it got stronger.'

Dawn realised, with uncanny perception, that there was something very deep but unacknowledged going on between these two gifted people – who Dawn thought were oddly reluctant or hesitant to take it beyond pure friendship: Jennifer's cool composure versus Ade's own form of shyness, if you like. Dawn has described Ade as 'funny, complex and profound'. The same words might be used to describe Jennifer, too.

'John Cleese said that people with similar backgrounds match intuitively,' said Ade of his early courting days with Jennifer. 'Jennifer was also a Forces kid, so was Dawn. I'll admit I had an enormous crush on Jennifer for some time before I owned up to her. I think you can have passions that run very long and very slow.

'I had an irrepressible desire to be near her but it didn't go any further. It was complicated by other girlfriends and boyfriends. Missed timings and possible connections. Nothing either of us regretted,' said Ade.

Dawn, concerned about the snail-like pace of the relationship, decided to make it crystal clear to both her friends that it was time to do something about it. Now. Perhaps her own happiness with Lenny Henry had something to do with it. Perhaps she was just being... Dawn.

'If it hadn't been for Dawn, I don't know what would have happened,' said Jennifer later. 'I was completely stupid and didn't realise we should be together. She persuaded me, helped bring Ade and me together. When we stopped working with the boys, I realised I missed him. But it was Dawn who gave him the confidence to believe that if he tried something on with me, it might actually work. She was a sort of godmother to our relationship.'

Early in 1985, Peter Richardson got The Comic Strip gang together again to make their first full-length feature film, called *The Supergrass*. Part funded by Film 4, written and directed by Richardson and shot on location in south-west England, the film is the story of a somewhat guileless, nerdish young man, Dennis (played by Ade), who stupidly boasts to his punk girlfriend Andrea (Dawn French) of his fantasy life as a drug smuggler. Police overhear him and turn Dennis into a 'supergrass'.

The Supergrass has its comic moments – Alexei Sayle, as usual, is superbly comic as Perryman, a sarky motor-cycle cop – yet what makes it all especially memorable is this: during the making of this movie, as they acted alongside each other, Ade and Jennifer finally threw caution to the wind – and started to really get to know each other. Properly.

As Jennifer recalled: 'We weren't an item until *The Supergrass*: it just seemed right at the time – logical. It was very romantic, lots of holding hands and roses. Before *The*

50

Supergrass we both had boyfriends and girlfriends so there was never a moment when we were both unattached.'

Jennifer plays the cool, aloof Lesley, an undercover cop-cum-femme fatale, tasked with keeping an eye on Dennis while working for her detective ex-lover Harvey (played by Peter Richardson). With Robbie Coltrane, Michael Elphick, Nigel Planer and Keith Allen in supporting roles, *The Supergrass* eventually received somewhat mixed reviews when first screened at the end of 1985, although it continues to have a big cult following.

In *The Supergrass*, however, there is no mistaking the on-screen chemistry between Ade and Jennifer in their many scenes together. Both in their late twenties, both extremely good-looking and charismatic, Jennifer seems to have that very special, very sexy 'glow' about her persona. It's unmistakably the glow of a woman who has fallen madly in love. (With a little help, of course, from a very 1980s big, blond, streaked, mullet-type hairdo.) Ade too looks love-struck and dreamy. OK, he's playing a pretty dumb guy, but he too has that slightly daft, squiffy look of a man totally smitten.

And so, in looking back at Jennifer's early career, *The Supergrass* stands out for one very good reason: it marked the beginning of what would, in time, develop into a long and happy marriage, one of the most successful and enduring in British show business. A case of art imitating life. Or the other way round.

The year 1985 proved to be a momentous one for Jennifer in many ways. Yet one day stands out – Saturday, 11 May – when Jennifer and Ade walked down the aisle in a small northern country church to make their wedding vows.

It was a typically low-key affair. A small group of friends and family gathered around them to celebrate the day. 'We got married in the village in Cheshire where Jennifer's parents lived,' recalled Ade.

'Jools Holland played the organ in the church. And Rik Mayall was the best man. I got a costume lady to take me out to get an Edwardian frock coat because I didn't want to wear Moss Bros shite.'

You only have to look at their wedding-day photograph to see the couple's happiness. And Ade has acknowledged that the song that means the most to him is called '$1000 Wedding' sung by Gram Parsons and Emmylou Harris: 'Jennifer introduced me to country music when we were courting and this was one of those songs. We still sing it in the car. I'm Gram and Jennifer is Emmylou.'

The newlyweds honeymooned on the romantic Caribbean island of St Lucia. 'We had already booked a holiday, so we decided to call it a honeymoon,' explained Ade.

'There are two little volcanic hills in St Lucia called the Pitons. Our hotel was just nestled inside them. I had a burger with thousand island dressing and got food poisoning and thought I was going to die. I was in the toilet for three days.'

But despite this somewhat unfortunate beginning, the rest of the honeymoon was as idyllic as they had hoped. And by late summer, Jennifer and Ade were thrilled to discover they were expecting their first child.

'We'd reached a time in our lives when we'd both got

very broody and lots of our friends were having babies,' said Jennifer.

No two women experience pregnancy in exactly the same way. Jennifer continued to work steadily throughout her first pregnancy, writing scripts with Dawn, yet there were times when, as Dawn put it, 'Things like hormones happen'.

'We said, "OK, let's just keep writing until you have the baby." We were writing right up until she gave birth and she'd cry and shout a lot. She apologised afterwards saying: "I just don't know where I've been." I knew it was madness because it was not at all like her,' said Dawn.

The autumn of 1985 brought Jennifer to a very big TV audience for the first time. For over 18 months, she and Dawn had been working intermittently on a sitcom, based on their flat-sharing experiences as students and written in collaboration with Ruby Wax and Tracey Ullman. Ben Elton was script editor. The stop-start nature of the project was mainly due to television companies' initial caution over commissioning the show.

Described at first as a female equivalent of *The Young Ones*, the sitcom *Girls on Top* was finally given the green light by ITV. And this time, there was no late-night screening: on 23 October 1985, the first series of *Girls on Top* was launched – 8.30pm, Wednesday night, and for seven successive weeks.

Comparisons with *The Young Ones* abounded but they were not exactly accurate: there was no extreme slapstick or camera tricks in this hellish scenario of four very different personalities living together in a couple of rooms in a London flat, advancing their own aims while simultaneously exploiting each other.

In fact, it had all started at a Christmas party thrown by Dawn and Jennifer's agent, where they met Ruby Wax for the first time and got into a conversation about the idea of an all-female flat-sharing sitcom.

Ruby Wax played Shelley DuPont, a brash, greedy, loud-mouthed American drama student, big on ego but desperately short on talent. Dawn was Amanda Ripley, a bossy, left-wing feminist who worked for a magazine called *Spare Cheek* (Amanda insisted she hated men though she would have given up all her credibility if only a man had shown a flicker of interest in her), and Jennifer was Jennifer Marsh, a rather dozy, slow-witted girl, who needed Amanda to get by.

Into the flat-sharing chaos came Tracey Ullman (in the first series only) as Candice Valentine, a bitchy, manipulative liar, not above nicking stuff from her flatmates and their landlady, Joan Greenwood as Lady Chloe Carlton, a somewhat eccentric, gin-swilling and batty romantic novelist living in the flat downstairs. Guest appearances in the series included Robbie Coltrane, Helen Lederer, Alan Rickman, Simon Brint, Rowland Rivron, and Harriet Thorpe as Amanda's feminist pal.

Much of the humour in *Girls on Top* came from the personality clash between Shelley and Amanda, balanced against Jennifer's complete lack of awareness – of anything, really. And in many ways, the relationship between Amanda and Jennifer became the template for the duo's French and Saunders sketches, where bossy Dawn would dominate the more dreamy, malleable Jennifer.

Audiences adored it: some 13 to 16 million viewers watched *Girls on Top*. And just like *The Young Ones*, *Girls on Top* ended after the second series ran in the autumn of 1986. (The house – and everyone in it – was blown to smithereens in the final episode, *Young Ones*-style, leaving no chance of any further series.) But by this time Jennifer and Dawn were well on their way to being mainstream TV performers. And the series had established women at the very forefront of mainstream television comedy: it was obvious – they were just as funny as the men.

Around the same time that *Girls on Top* went out, the duo made their debut on BBC1 in *Happy Families*. Penned by Ben Elton and produced by Paul Jackson (who had also produced *Girls on Top*), the six-part serial told the story of the search for four missing girls from one dysfunctional family – the Fuddles – as their grandmother, Edith, 89, approached the end of her life.

Essentially a bizarre female version of the 1949 classic black comedy movie *Kind Hearts and Coronets*, *Happy Families* was a star vehicle for Jennifer, who played both Edith and her four granddaughters: a Hollywood soap actress, a jailbird, a nun and a French girl living in a commune.

It was an innovative series – each sister's story was shot in a different style. Ade played the girls' batty brother, Guy, with Dawn in a cameo role as a flour-stained cook, Stephen Fry as a pompous doctor and Helen Lederer as the family's maid Flossie, with appearances from Hugh Laurie, Una Stubbs and Jim Broadbent.

It wasn't a ratings winner. Yet Jennifer was especially good as Cassie, the glamorous, self-centred Hollywood star, in what was essentially a spoof on a *Dallas*-type TV soap setting.

'There are two mes inside here. There's a little girl who says: "Hey, look at me, I'm a superstar." But then there's a very quiet and sincere person who says: "Hang on, hold back, remember you are a talented person. Do something worthwhile,"' says Cassie of her life as a star.

Perhaps writer Ben Elton was sending up overindulged TV soap stars, Hollywood-style. Or did Jennifer, already conscious of the difficulty of retaining a private place in a very public world, pen those lines? It's an interesting thought.

Happy Families is a testament to Jennifer's acting skill and her good looks. She makes the switch from each different role with considerable ease. And, of course, playing an 89-year-old means a great deal of help from the makeup department. Elaborate sections of rubber Latex had to be applied to her face, neck and hands.

'Three hours every morning to put it all on. The good thing is peeling it off in one lump – and there's Edith Fuddle's old face in the wastepaper basket,' she said at the time, unaware that these three-hour sessions in the makeup chair were due to become a regular feature of her working life in the years ahead when French and Saunders took off.

Although Dawn had a small role to play in *Happy Families*, this was really the first time that Jennifer had demonstrated her talents as a solo performer, creating a template for their future: they would always separate and pair up again at different times.

They had already decided at this early stage that separate projects were to their advantage: the experiences would help them bring more into their comedy performance when they reunited.

'It was important because some people thought it hard to think of us individually,' said Jennifer.

That might have been the case at the time, but this decision, nearly 30 years ago, is yet another noteworthy aspect of their careers: it's rare enough to create a successful female double act. Victoria Wood and Julie Walters worked together, to great success, at one point in the 1990s, but essentially their huge popularity is derived from their careers as separate, highly talented performers.

At the time, however, there were other, even more important developments in Jennifer's and Ade's lives: on 22 January 1986, their first daughter, Eleanor 'Ella' Rose, arrived. For a short time, Jennifer's working life took a back seat, though motherhood also coincided with a turning point for her: the realisation that what had started out as a lark was now developing into a proper showbiz career.

'Six years in and you start thinking: "This is what I'm going to do for the rest of my life,"' she recalled later.

On New Year's Day 1986, Channel 4 screened *The Comic Strip Presents... Consuela*, a 45-minute spoof on the Hitchcock movie *Rebecca*, co-written by Jennifer and Dawn.

And in March, Jennifer and Dawn were invited onto Channel 4's *Saturday Live*, an innovative comedy and music show that went out before a youthful audience as a showcase for new comedy and musical talents. Their sketch, with Jennifer as a muddled, sharp-talking TV producer and Dawn as her sidekick on the studio floor, was an indicator of the shape of things to come: two women mocking TV types and personalities at work, mercilessly sending up their insecurities and shortcomings.

That April, Jennifer and Dawn were on stage again, performing at the Shaftesbury Theatre in London for the very first televised fundraising effort for Comic Relief, the beginning of a long-term commitment to deploying their talents to raise money for charity.

Comic Relief was founded by scriptwriter Richard Curtis and Lenny Henry, not long after Bob Geldof's amazing, ground-breaking Band Aid initiative to raise awareness of and money for starving children in Africa. Launched live from a refugee camp in Sudan on Christmas Day 1985 on BBC1, the Comic Relief charity was born following the news that a devastating famine had crippled Ethiopia, and something had to be done to help.

The idea behind Comic Relief was simple: get a whole bunch of much-loved British comedians to make people laugh as a way of raising money to help those in desperate need, both in the UK and overseas.

That first ever televised Comic Relief fundraising show in April went out on BBC1 as a compilation of three live Comic Relief concerts staged at the Shaftesbury Theatre, London, in the spring of 1986.

Since then, Comic Relief, Children in Need and Sport Relief have become the most high-profile show business fundraising events on BBC TV. (The highlight is the biennial Red Nose Day, held in March and alternating with Sport Relief.)

Jennifer and Dawn were on stage at the Shaftesbury Theatre in that first ever fundraiser alongside many of their

Comic Strip colleagues, as well as stars such as Rowan Atkinson, Billy Connolly and Ronnie Corbett. The star turn was Cliff Richard and *The Young Ones* performing the song 'Living Doll'. The new version of the song went on to top the charts in seven different countries – and made millions for Comic Relief.

However, for new parents Jennifer and Ade there were more surprises in store: by the autumn, Jennifer was pregnant with their second child. And they were busy juggling domestic life in west London with their respective writing and performing commitments.

'We're a very contented couple, but not complacent. I worry constantly and get anxious; Jennifer is very calm. We're adult enough to tell each other when we think something is rubbish, but we rarely talk about work at home. Life's about other things, isn't it?' said Ade at the time.

It's a sensible philosophy, one that would work well for their marriage over the years. But at that point, there were certain 'other things' ahead in Jennifer's career that would prove to be a huge talking point for TV critics – and audiences – all over the country.

The BBC were poised to sign up French and Saunders for their own series on television. Very soon, a more mainstream audience would be watching the double act that had started out as a joke, a bit of a student laugh.

And although she would go on to build up a larger audience with every passing year, Jennifer was determined to keep the two sides of her life – the public and the personal – as distinctly separate as possible. Fame was on its way. Just two years married and with a growing family, she was about to experience the roller-coaster ride of wide public acclaim.

And with typical Jennifer Saunders' cool, she would, of course, manage to take it all – the ups and downs – completely in her stride.

CHAPTER 3

FRENCH AND SAUNDERS

The year 1987 was the year that launched *Fatal Attraction* and Rick Astley ('Never Gonna Give You Up'), ushered in Maggie Thatcher's final term as Prime Minister – and gave the UK its worst ever storm in history. And any television viewer who had never heard of Jennifer Saunders but happened to catch the first ever *French and Saunders* series for BBC2, which went out at 9pm on 9 March 1987, might easily have wondered who these girls were – and whether they were meant to be funny.

The first series of *French and Saunders* consisted of six consecutive 30-minute weekly shows. It was not a runaway success. There were sketches and spoof documentaries that both Jennifer and Dawn wrote and performed, but the format for the first series was somewhat odd: a mocked-up TV variety show being performed in front of a studio audience, heard but never seen. It didn't quite work.

The general idea of the fake show was to have Jennifer and Dawn presenting the entertainment (some bad dancers called the 'Hot Hoofers', with bongos and keyboard music by Raw Sex (Rowland Rivron and Simon Brint)), interspersed with scenes of the girls arguing backstage or playing behind-the-scenes characters such as wardrobe ladies. In between, they performed their sketches.

The overall effect was unsatisfactory, a little bit tacky. Yet there was innovation too, and a format that would serve them well in the future. Each show featured a special guest playing themselves: Alison Moyet, Roy Castle, Michael Grade, Julie T. Wallace, Joan Armatrading, Jools Holland, Rik Mayall and Harry (soon to be 'Loadsamoney') Enfield all turned up in the first series.

This was unusual, even a bit daring for television at that time. Using celebrities as themselves as laughter bait is commonplace now – the bigger the name, the more the audience laps it up, and Morecambe & Wise, the nation's most revered double act, had proved its comic value back in the seventies – but it still wasn't as commonplace then. Typically, in the fourth show, Jennifer and Dawn attempted to convince guest Michael Grade, who was then Managing Director of BBC Television, not to drop their programme. As if...

'It wasn't received particularly well. The ratings were not great. But new comedy shows usually aren't well received,' recalled Patrick Stoddart, former *Sunday Times* TV critic and interviewer. 'Even *Fawlty Towers* didn't get huge ratings at first, and the first *Blackadder* went down the toilet – and you've got to remember that The Comic Strip was a cult thing. 'So when French and Saunders started out, people weren't saying: "Oh good, those two have got together for the series."'

Stoddart's view was that two women, both genuinely funny in their own right, could only be a good thing for TV comedy.

'There was a growing enthusiasm for them, even though there were reviewers back then who were very suspicious of funny women. That first series was a bit tentative, not as confident and assured as what came later, but it had enough funny material in it, and they didn't have to find anything about each other. But they were still trying to find out what worked for them and TV.'

Stoddart also points out that this was the first time the pair had to make their own decisions on what the audience would find funny.

'With The Comic Strip, Peter Richardson had a very clear idea of how he wanted those films to be. So that first time was scary for any woman out to prove themselves times 10.'

Jennifer has admitted that making the *French and Saunders* early series presented certain challenges for the duo. They had very definite ideas about what they wanted, and their work on *The Comic Strip Presents* movies was very much a collaborative group effort, with Peter Richardson helming the proceedings. Finding themselves working for the key mainstream TV broadcaster was a somewhat different proposition, though.

'Our first series was not good, but we were very cocky then – "We know what to do" – we made some very big errors,' said Jennifer. 'In some ways Dawn and I are probably more difficult to work with than a lot of people on television; we're a lot more demanding. I hate it if you've spent so much time writing something only to have the joke edited out because someone doesn't understand it or they're too rushed.'

Dawn has admitted that they were fortunate that the BBC were supportive of them after the first series and gave them time to develop their act.

'Our first series was tricky and we were finding our feet, but Jim Moir, the Controller at that point, had faith,' she recalled.

Patrick Stoddart feels that a big part of the secret of Jennifer's subsequent success lies in her acting ability and the way she can adapt, switching around from one character to another. 'Jennifer's versatility has always struck me – she can do three or four different roles, all ages; she can act and be funny in lots of different ways. She's versatile in her humour too, not just her acting – much more of a chameleon.'

In a face-to-face interview-type situation, Stoddart always found Jennifer to be very open: 'Given the on-screen persona, which is quite cold at times, she's not at all like that. She's funny, articulate and very thoughtful. And definitely attractive. I find intelligence and wit attractive – she has them both.

Some people are daunted by the thought of encountering Jennifer Saunders; they assume she'll be remote and razor-toothed. 'She's not that person at all. She might well be razor-toothed if pushed, but she gives the impression that it would take a very hard shove indeed to rattle the Saunders' equilibrium.'

As Jennifer and Ade awaited the birth of their second child that spring, perhaps there were moments when their equilibrium as writers and performers might have been rattled somewhat. Showbiz, for all its glitter and shiny surface, is a tough, often brutal, world behind the scenes. And TV comedy, no matter how talented the performer or writer, can sometimes be a hit-and-miss affair for reasons beyond the control of those creating it.

Ade's BBC2 reunion early in 1987 with his *Young Ones/Comic Strip* collaborators Rik Mayall and Nigel Planer, in the sitcom *Filthy, Rich & Catflap*, written by Ben Elton, didn't emulate the cult success of *The Young Ones*. A send-up of show business and celebrity culture but with some of the raw, slapstick, over-the-top humour of *The Young Ones*, the show was reasonably well received, but, somewhat inexplicably, it ran for just one series.

Another anarchic comedy series, *Hardwicke House*, made by Central Television and set in a lawless inner-city comprehensive (in which Rik and Ade were billed as two ex-pupils recently released from borstal), hit the decks after just two episodes were shown on ITV, even though a series of seven episodes had been filmed. (Rik and Ade's episodes, alas, were never screened.)

Much mystery surrounds the controversy over *Hardwicke House*. Both the press and the public complained about it vociferously after the first episode aired in February 1987, claiming it was too offensive. But why it was taken off so abruptly – highly unusual for any TV series anywhere – has never been fully explained; the writers and performers had been contracted and paid for a second series, which unfortunately never happened.

So Ade and Jennifer, though seen as youthful comic performers on TV with bright futures, would have had much to ponder that spring. Audiences see the end product and judge accordingly. But for the entertainers and writers, the behind-the-scenes creation of the material is one huge leap of faith: like acting, comedy is a risky enterprise. You put yourself on the line every time.

'I think unless you have a huge ego you will never get rid of that fear. You need an enormous one in order to convince yourself that what you've done is brilliant,' said Jennifer. 'Even when people say "it's great", you say "thank you" but you know in your heart of hearts that what you're doing is... well, I always think if I have done it, then it can't be all that great. You know, it's this thing of everyone else being more clever.'

Yet in June 1987, when Jennifer gave birth to her second daughter, Beatrice Louise ('Beattie'), such insecurities could be put to one side. With an 18-month-old Ella and a new baby at home plus two TV careers to juggle, the pair had their hands full, although they were as delighted and besotted with their new arrival as anyone can be: 'Quite simply, the best baby that ever was,' as Ade crowed at the time.

The first BBC2 series of *French and Saunders* had pulled in 5 million viewers (a respectable figure at that time), but when Jennifer returned to the BBC to work with Dawn on the second series at the end of 1987, it was decided that they would ditch the variety show format and focus on their sketches while continuing to torment their celebrity guests, of course. And before the new series went out, there were other film and TV appearances.

Eat the Rich, the second full-length *Comic Strip Presents* movie, was also released at the end of 1987. Jennifer appeared as Lady Caroline, Dawn as Debbie Draws and Ade as Charles.

An anti-Thatcher satire (a transsexual waiter starts a mini revolution), the film was universally panned. *The Sunday Times* dubbed it 'riddled with left-wing bias' and its release in the US fared little better, although *The New York Times* review by Vincent Canby was kinder – 'engaging exuberance and a number of low comedy gags'.

However, *The Strike*, a *Comic Strip Presents* special which went out on Channel 4 in February 1988, proved a much better proposition. The 59-minute satirical tale of how a British screenwriter (Alexei Sayle) sells Hollywood a script about the British miners' strike of 1984 is an acerbic spoof on Hollywood and LA's values. (Naturally, the Hollywood moguls insist that the miners win the strike in order to have an audience-friendly, upbeat ending.)

With Peter Richardson as Al Pacino playing Arthur Scargill, Jennifer as Meryl Streep playing Scargill's wife and Robbie Coltrane as a cigar-chomping movie mogul, *The Strike* won a Rose d'Or (Golden Rose) award at the 1988 Montreux Festival (the broadcasting industry's most prestigious international award for entertainment programmes) and is generally regarded as one of the most successful and entertaining of all the *Comic Strip Presents* films.

Jennifer's role involved some clever research. 'The peeling of the orange when I was playing Meryl playing Mrs Scargill was based on something I read about Streep, that she had this knack for pulling focus, even when she didn't have a line in the scene,' she said.

Good point. Mrs Scargill's (or Meryl's) scene with a sleepless, bare-chested Arthur/Al supping a beer and complaining how everyone hates him while she calmly peels the orange is superbly timed, a real scene stealer – and a perfect example of Jennifer's forensic observational powers as a performer. And *The Strike* itself is a good example of how The Comic Strip's output, despite its hit-and-miss approach, was a unique proposition right from the start, simply because Richardson and The Comic Strip group were given the freedom, back in the 1980s, to do what they believed worked best.

In February 1988, Dawn and Jennifer appeared in *A Night of Comic Relief* on BBC1, the first ever Red Nose Day telethon, which raised more than £13 million. A sketch involving the duo and Michael Buerk caused controversy when Dawn said to Buerk: 'I'm Dawn, you f***ing ninny!'. Afterwards, Dawn denied using the four-letter word.

The second series of *French and Saunders* went out on BBC2 in March 1988. With a much more loosely constructed format, the girls' unique brand of humour in their sketches and send-ups started to come through. There was a hilarious spoof of television, with the duo running their own breakfast TV station, and their ongoing adolescent sketches involving two teenage girls, seen in the first series – 'you might be a homo sapiens' was a typical line – but now talking about contraception, is classic *French and Saunders* with its lines about 'Philippine tubes' and doctors 'inserting UFOs inside you', material that, for those times, was still regarded as quite bold – and would probably not have been permitted on TV even a few years earlier.

Guest appearances were from Joan Bakewell, Squeeze, Toyah Willcox, Ben Elton, Lulu, Kirsty MacColl, June Whitfield and, in the penultimate show, Jennifer and Dawn's respective real-life husbands, Ade and Lenny, also appeared alongside them in a dinner party spoof reminiscent of the Mike Leigh hit play, *Abigail's Party*. This time, the series was deemed a real success. The *French and Saunders*' audience was growing.

'People who have never seen them before are waking up to their talent at last,' said the BBC at the time.

And it wasn't just the UK audiences. By now, *French and Saunders* had attracted the attention of the makers of a US/UK TV production for *Muppets*' creator Jim Henson's company. Called *The Storyteller*, with a screenplay by Anthony Minghella, this was a children's TV series using actors and puppets to recreate various European folk tales.

Dawn and Jennifer were perfectly cast as two fabulously bad sisters, clad in voluminous taffeta, in an episode called 'Sapsorrow', named after the girls' beautiful good sister in a Cinderella-type story. The episode aired on Channel 4 in July 1988 and was also screened in the US on Home Box Office earlier that year.

Yet controversy was never far away from the duo's work. Two of their most memorable *French and Saunders* creations, the 'fat old men' (the sexist lager slobs on the sofa), generated a wave of protest from BBC viewers when they appeared in the *French and Saunders* Christmas special 1988.

The fuss was mostly about the two men's ribald comments on the royals: Dawn's old man grunted that the Queen wasn't like her sister Margaret, 'who goes like a bunny.' Jennifer's old man followed this up by saying: 'Queen or no Queen, she's got a woman's needs.' Perhaps a tad outrageous back then, but nonetheless, it caused as much laughter as eyebrow-raising. But it was still the Thatcherite 1980s, and Tory MP Anthony Beaumont-Dark said the sketch was 'pathetic and offensive filth'. He demanded that the BBC launch an enquiry. They didn't, of course.

The biggest laugh of the Christmas special came from the girls' legendary Bananarama send-up, calling themselves Lananeeneenoonoo (joined by Kathy Burke). So successful was the Bananarama sketch, they considered releasing the song, but decided it wasn't a winner. They changed their minds when they learnt that the all-girl band loved the spoof so much they would happily agree to team up with Jennifer, Kathy and Dawn to make a record: 'Help', which went on to raise millions for Comic Relief.

'Bananarama were really wild party girls, we couldn't keep up,' Jennifer later recalled.

Around this time, with their audience growing as quickly as their two young daughters, Jennifer and Ade tried moving briefly from west London to the peace and tranquillity of the

Somerset countryside. But work commitments made full-time country life unrealistic and so they moved back to a family house amidst the green and pleasant spaces of London's Richmond Hill.

By the beginning of 1989, Jennifer was on the road on tour – the first time she and Dawn had been touring since Comic Strip days.

Promoter Phil McIntyre had recognised that the pair had established a considerable following around the country, especially amongst younger women, and he persuaded them to embark on their first full-scale solo tour of the UK.

'People love a double act,' said McIntyre. 'If you're a double act it's like being a footballer who's left-footed, you've got a bit of an advantage because there aren't as many of you. And also, they're women, so there's a double rarity, like being a left-footer who's really fast.'

The tour, *An Evening with French and Saunders*, went to 31 provincial theatres, winding up with a four-week run at London's Shaftesbury Theatre. It was a sell-out, much to Jennifer's surprise, thanks, in part, to their growing TV popularity: 'We thought it was going to be horrible. When you book a tour you don't know how it's going to go. A lot of stuff used to be fairly intimate so we never used to think we could convey to a big theatre full of people. But we're playing to at least 2,000 people a night.'

The live show opened with about 20 minutes of Raw Sex with Rowland Rivron and Simon Brint, then included cracks about Janet Street-Porter and their friend Ruby Wax; a chat with a famous actress, Wendy Dench, sketches about Madonna and Claire Rayner in a steam bath, and lots of digs at pop group fans. And Dawn sending round collection buckets into the audience for chocolate. Most of the material was brand new, though the theme of adolescence remained, as it had in the TV series – very much part of their act.

A live show, of course, means a different rehearsal discipline. Improvisation, always part of their repertoire, had to be incorporated after they'd worked out their ideas, rather than just writing and then memorising lines. And their audience, by this time, was crossing all age groups – lots of young teenage girls as well as their parents. And middle-aged couples. Family audiences in 2,000-seater venues. Half-hour sessions after the show signing autographs and programmes for the fans. All a far cry from their audiences in the early days, the drunken Comedy Store crowd – or the feminist crew who took alternative comedy seriously and wanted ranting polemic rather than wry humour and childish, but very effective, parody.

With the live tour acknowledged to be a big success, family life in Richmond took centre stage again. Yet motherhood for Jennifer was not quite how she had imagined it to be.

'You always think your kids will somehow belong to you, that you can mould them into something, that they will reflect you. But they don't – they're individuals from the day they're born. Ella's such a little person and she has such a complete dress sense.

'She'll say "Mummy, you're not very pretty" because I'm wearing old jeans. She'll ask: "Why are you wearing them? You're not a boy." She wants me to wear dresses with pretty bows on. And she's so particular about colours and things – completely unlike me.'

The couple had some help at home but the Edmondson household was run on fairly traditional lines.

'I have a nanny who comes in daily, but I do everything. Sometimes I wish I didn't but then it's just in my nature to do domestic things. Sometimes I think I should be sitting at my desk being creative and all that. But instead I'm wondering where I can get a massive fridge from that'll be big enough to hold two weeks' shopping from Sainsbury's.

'Ade's great at tiling, wallpapering, decorating, carpentry. He's brilliant at it and loves it. He says if he wasn't doing what he does, he'd be a carpenter. He's a "doer". Me, I'm a procrastinator.'

With more and more people recognising her, Jennifer's feelings about maintaining her privacy still remained the same. She simply felt uncomfortable with that kind of attention.

'I don't like being recognised. I'm quite shy and I don't like people looking at me. I hate those scenes at the cash till when someone says: "Oh yes, I thought it was you." Then they go off and get someone else and say: "Look, it's that one off the telly."

'My greatest ambition is to be very good on film and I'd have loved to be a *real* pop star. I'd just love to go up on stage and make so much noise people can't even hear what they're thinking.'

When you consider where her career would eventually take her, this desire to make a racket doesn't sound all that unusual, even if it is very much at variance with Jennifer's wish to remain unnoticed when not performing. Yet whatever her secret ambitions at the time, one theme that would run consistently through Jennifer's life would be her constant commitment to helping others.

As well as an ongoing involvement with Comic Relief since its inception, there would be any number of fundraising projects and charity involvements over time – but, in 1989, Jennifer's role co-directing *The Secret Policeman's Biggest Ball*, the all-star benefit to raise funds for the human rights organisation Amnesty International, made headlines as a first: the first time a woman had directed such a big comedy enterprise for charity.

John Cleese, who already had a long-term commitment to Amnesty (he suggested the first *Secret Policeman's Ball* in the 1970s and was the driving force behind several such concerts), approached Jennifer to co-direct. She was delighted.

'I thought it would be good for me. I often back away from things. This isn't like directing a play, it's a matter of organising and helping people,' she explained at the time. 'And it's an awareness thing. People should know that they [Amnesty] are still there doing good work, still requiring donations.'

Previous Amnesty fundraisers had focused on music. This time, *The Secret Policeman's Biggest Ball* benefit shows, performed over four nights in August and September 1989 at the Cambridge Theatre in London, were all about comedy. There were appearances from Cleese, Michael Palin, Peter Cook and Dudley Moore, John Bird, Stephen Fry, Hugh Laurie, Lenny Henry, Rory Bremner, Kathy

Burke, Ben Elton, Robbie Coltrane, Willie Rushton and the *Spitting Image* puppets.

Jennifer and Dawn performed an improvised sketch as roadies and their familiar 'Schoolgirl Contraception' skit, with Dawn performing a supercharged brief solo called 'I'm a Dancer'. Ade joined John Cleese for a hilariously funny sketch called 'The Last Supper' with Cleese as the Pope and Ade as his hapless employee, Michelangelo. The fundraiser was a huge success and was eventually screened on ITV in October that year.

Essentially, it had been down to the directors to help persuade or cajole their famous friends to appear for free. And despite Jennifer's initial concerns, the eventual roll call on stage was a virtual who's who of British comedy at the time.

'The turnout was terrific. I thought there'd only be three people who'd want to do it,' she admitted later.

Later that year, Jennifer and Dawn started work on the third series of *French and Saunders* for the BBC. Although this series was to prove their most successful so far, they initially struggled to come up with ideas they believed would work. Only with the final deadline fast approaching did they eventually get through.

The year had also involved more location filming with Peter Richardson's Comic Strip ensemble for a *Comic Strip Presents* movie, *GLC*. This was a spoof of the former Greater London Council, shot as a Hollywood avenger film. Robbie Coltrane starred as Charles Bronson/Ken Livingstone and Jennifer played Brigitte Nielsen as the Ice Maiden, a blonde female prime minister.

GLC was well received when it went out on Channel 4 on 15 February 1990. TV critic Mark Lawson said: '*GLC* was hugely funny and tightly produced. The way Saunders' accent included both the Nielsen Scandinavian and the Thatcher lispy husk was typical of the intricacy of the design.'

The third series of *French and Saunders*, which went out as seven weekly episodes from 15 March to 26 April 1990 on BBC2, was primarily a series of send-ups of movie favourites. It worked brilliantly. Ten million viewers tuned in, doubling the success of their previous series.

They satirised *The Sound of Music*, *The Exorcist* and *Gone with the Wind*, and the series included the especially classic parody of *What Ever Happened to Baby Jane?*, where Dawn played the Bette Davis character and Jennifer the crippled Joan Crawford.

'I think by the third series we'd really got the hang of it and became mainstream,' Jennifer admitted.

But it was in the sixth episode of this series that the seed was sown for Jennifer's future: a sketch called 'Modern Mother and Daughter' portrayed Jennifer as a crazy, hippie, party-loving mother, with Dawn as her incredibly prim and sensible Goody Two Shoes daughter. No one could know this at the time, of course, but the brief skit was the genesis of something much, much bigger. And it would change the course of Jennifer's life and career for good.

But all this was in the future; the spring of 1990 had brought the Edmondsons another welcome surprise: soon, there would be another addition to their family of two girls.

Ade, who definitely wanted a girl – 'from what I've seen,

boys are aggressive, nasty little creatures' – was starring as Brad Majors in a big West End revival of *The Rocky Horror Show* at the Piccadilly Theatre that summer – while Jennifer made a brief guest appearance, complete with stripy top and gold dangly earrings, on BBC2's *Rita Rudner* show, which aired later in the year. (Rudner, a well-known US stand-up comedienne, was given her own comedy series but it ended after just six episodes.)

While awaiting the birth of her third child, Jennifer continued to join forces with other comic talents. She paired with Ruby Wax to present an episode of Ruby's popular BBC show, *The Full Wax*, and, since both women were pregnant at the time the series was filmed, the hilarious episode featuring Jennifer and Zsa Zsa Gabor made full comic use of the situation: 'I'm with egg, Jennifer is football stadium,' quipped Ruby. (The episode, screened in the first series of *The Full Wax*, went out on the BBC in January 1991.)

Jennifer spent the final weeks of her pregnancy on location in Polperro, Cornwall, for her role in the film adaptation of Beatrix Potter's famous children's story, *The Tale of Little Pig Robinson*. This tells the story of a gullible pig called Robinson, who is 'pignapped' on his way to market and winds up marooned on a desert island.

Alongside an all-star cast which included Timothy Spall, Thora Hird, Edward Fox, Toyah Willcox, Prunella Scales and *'Allo Allo!* star Gorden Kaye, Jennifer and Dawn played piglet Robinson's aunts, Miss Dorcas and Miss Porcas.

Playing a pig was not exactly fun, especially in sticky

summer temperatures – and that summer of 1990 was a notably hot one. It involved being in makeup by 5.30am each morning, to be fitted with a black Latex-rubber pig snout, and then being encased in voluminous flowery skirts and shawls complete with nylon and foam padding.

Jennifer was, by now, accustomed to long sessions in the makeup department – the third series of *French and Saunders* had involved the duo spending several hours in makeup to create some of their characters (three hours in the makeup chair to become the two big, hardy old countrywomen who refuse to make a fuss about anything, even losing a limb in agricultural machinery), but it was especially uncomfortable for someone in the later months of pregnancy. Reason enough, perhaps, for Jennifer's reluctance to give any on-set interviews to journalists, other than commenting: 'I've been a pig all my life.'

The Edmondsons' third daughter, Freya Domenica, arrived on 16 October 1990.

'I'd have loved one boy but I'm very happy with my girls,' she said afterwards. 'I've seen people with boys and they're much wilder. With three girls I'm hoping to have the cast of a Chekhov play. Or perhaps the new Supremes.'

Chore-wise, Ade happily took over many of the domestic tasks, including cooking, after Freya arrived, before pairing up again with Rik Mayall to co-write the sitcom *Bottom* for BBC2, one of the channel's biggest ever comedy hits.

'He's better than me and he does it without making a point of it, which is quite exceptional. When I was pregnant last time I couldn't even boil a kettle. I left a haddock on the stove for six hours and set fire to a wooden spoon,' recalled

A young Jennifer during *The Comic Strip Presents…* years. ©*Rex Features*

A strong bond.

From the early eighties to the present day, Dawn French and Jennifer have proved to be a
successful comedy duo.

Jennifer and husband Adrian Edmondson, a fellow comedian, have been married for over 25 years.

©Rex Features

Co-star of *Girls on Top* Ruby Wax with Jennifer and Adrian in 1989.

Jennifer's career has taken her down many roads, and she has worked with a number of different celebrities and artists on various shows, sketches, films and plays.

Above: From left: Hugh Laurie, Emma Freud, Stephen Fry, Jennifer and Tony Slattery in 1991.
                                                                          ©Getty Images

Below: From left: Jennifer Saunders, Antonio Banderas, Mike Myers and Cameron Diaz. *Shrek 2,* Cannes Film Festival, 2004.
                                                                          ©Getty Images

Jennifer's various guises.

Above left: From left: Dawn French, Jennifer and Ruby with Joan Greenwood (below).
Girls on Top, 1985. ©*Rex Features*

Above right: As Edina Monsoon with fashion model Marie Helvin. ©*Getty Images*

Below: On stage with Dawn for the final UK performance of *French & Saunders
Still Alive*. ©*Getty Images*

Jennifer and her daughters.

Jennifer. 'Now, when I go into the kitchen I hear: "Don't go near the cooker, you'll just burn something."'

As 1990 drew to a close, there was more good news on the career front: *French and Saunders* had won a prestigious Writers' Guild of Great Britain Award for Best Light Entertainment on TV, the first of many industry awards. *Little Pig Robinson* went out on ITV on Boxing Day 1990 to general acclaim. And by early 1991, the two women were contemplating the next series of *French and Saunders*.

By now, they had established a working routine for the series, preferring to go out to work in a small office at BBC Television Centre while leaving their respective domestic lives at home: with a nanny to help with the three girls and Ade able to juggle his own working commitments as he and Rik wrote *Bottom*, this suited Jennifer best.

'If I worked from home I'd get nothing done. I'd be staring at the wall thinking: "Hmm... that colour, why did I choose it? I must go out and get a colour chart this very minute."'

Yet as the two women started to map out ideas for the fourth series, they were sharing a very big secret. One they were resolutely determined would remain hidden from everyone. Especially the press.

Because while Jennifer and Ade's world away from the TV studios revolved around a noisy, cheerful household with three fair-haired little girls to love and nurture, Dawn and Lenny, despite their successful careers, had been quietly nursing a secret heartache for some time.

They longed to be parents, to enjoy the same kind of

family life the Edmondsons had; they had everything to give. But after seven years of marriage, it just hadn't happened. As a consequence, the couple had taken the big step of approaching the adoption service: they wanted to adopt their own baby.

A rigorous, sometimes fraught process at the best of times, the pair's fame as TV stars did nothing at all to help them – for one thing, as performers they would be required to spend a certain amount of time working away from home, and while Dawn could easily point to Jennifer as a great friend and working partner who was a perfect role model, capably juggling the demands of a showbiz career with family life and enjoying the balance between work and home life, the wait for news from the adoption service was a nail-biter. And very, very painful, too.

'Nobody knew what we were going through except Jennifer, and she was very encouraging about it,' recalled Dawn. 'I knew I couldn't tell anyone because it would have got out. And I didn't want anything fouling up the process.'

In early spring 1991, Lenny and Dawn were told they had been given full approval to adopt a child; the major hurdle had been overcome. After that, it was a case of waiting. Yet the wait to hear that the adoption service had a suitable baby seemed to go on forever: spring turned to summer and summer to autumn without any news.

Both women understood perfectly that when the call did come, Dawn would be dropping everything immediately: this was a life-changing event. But until the call came, two careers were in limbo. Dawn held her breath waiting for that all-important call and Jennifer waited to see if any other work would turn up. But as she recalled: 'The phone didn't ring.'

However, in November that year, Dawn and Lenny finally got the call they had longed for: a two-week-old baby girl had been found for the couple. Amidst total secrecy, Dawn rushed off to meet their new daughter and take her home. And while the BBC's planning for the fourth series of *French and Saunders* was already underway, with studio space booked, director, producer and crew chosen, there was one major problem: the new series had not yet been written. Dawn was off the project. Unless something was done very quickly, the BBC would have a gaping hole in their schedule. And two careers would probably be on the line...

Jennifer is the sort of person who performs well under pressure: when the deadline is imminent, she stops gazing into space and goes for it big time. And in this situation, she proved herself to be immensely resourceful. Quick as a flash, she picked up on the potential of a project that would give Dawn the necessary breathing space to settle into motherhood and gave the BBC executives a new proposition: a brand-new idea to replace the *French and Saunders* series.

'What Jennifer did was simply say: "Right. We can't do the series and I'll do what I've been meaning to do for ages but have been too lazy to do. This'll give me the kick I need to write a sitcom. Therefore I don't have to explain too much because I'm going to be giving them a product,"' explained Dawn.

This ploy enabled Dawn to slip off quietly.

'No one said anything at all. But if it hadn't been for her, I wouldn't have been able to get away with it.'

That eleventh-hour 'product' turned out to be *Absolutely Fabulous*. Spotting the wider comic potential of the 12-minute 'Modern Mother and Daughter' sketch that she and Dawn had performed in the previous series of *French and Saunders* and taking it further, by creating a group of memorable characters around them, Jennifer was able to convince the BBC executives that the show would go on – only this time, the audience would be getting a different kind of Jennifer Saunders. This time, she'd be playing just one woman: Edina (or 'Eddy') Monsoon.

'I thought I could write this character. I knew her quite well – and the character could go further,' recalled Jennifer afterwards.

As she made her way back down the corridors of BBC Television Centre in west London after that all-important meeting with the executives, Jennifer must have felt immense relief that a solution had been found. Yet there was also a frisson of apprehension about the prospect of embarking on her first major solo project.

'I had to write everything myself for *Absolutely Fabulous* – I couldn't put it off and hope that Dawn would come up with the ideas. That's the good thing about being half of a partnership; there's always someone else to bully you. The problem is there's always someone else to blame.'

Edina Monsoon – divorced, neurotic, fashion victim in too-tight clothing and everyone's PR person from hell – was as over the top and wildly entertaining as any of Jennifer and Dawn's other creations. (The name itself,

Eddy Monsoon, is a play on Ade's surname, and he had already used it for a character appearing in a *Comic Strip Presents* movie. It was also the name Ade and Jennifer subsequently used for their production company, Mr and Mrs Monsoon Limited.)

But what neither Jennifer nor the BBC could have guessed after that auspicious meeting was that this time the character and the series were destined to take the TV world by storm – and turn Jennifer Saunders into a star writer and performer in her own right.

Dawn French has described the way Jennifer handled the situation at the BBC when her daughter Billie arrived as 'the act of a true friend'.

'I worried about how this kid would ever become mine and Jennifer said: "I've got three kids and I gave birth to them but I don't know who they are because they are all so different." That was a really great thing for me to know.'

There is no denying the fact that this incident cemented the already close relationship between the two women. And as for any gap in the proceedings as a double act, this was easily explained as a mutual decision: the ongoing need to work on separate projects.

It was two years before the real truth about the situation was revealed to the press – after Dawn had taken a year off to be with her daughter and then gone on to have a big success with *Murder Most Horrid*, a black comedy series on BBC2 in which she played a different character in every episode.

'There comes a point when you become so identified as a couple that the chances of employment outside the double act grow less and less, so we decided to give it a rest and see what turned up,' Jennifer said at the time.

What actually 'turned up' when she created Edina, Patsy and *Ab Fab* at that crisis point proved to be the most pivotal point in Jennifer's career. Whatever her own inner insecurities or concerns, she was about to light up the small screen as a female comic writer/performer like no other. The creation of Edina Monsoon would turn her into a global icon – and send the careers of her *Ab Fab* cohorts, Joanna Lumley, June Whitfield, Julia Sawalha and Jane Horrocks, into overdrive too.

In the comedy world, people often say that timing is everything. And the early 1990s was, without doubt, the perfect time to launch a TV series like *Ab Fab*, with its insider's peek into the worlds of PR, advertising, fashion, celebs and baby-boomer excess: no TV executive would have considered bringing Edina and Patsy and their booze and drug-taking antics into the living rooms of the nation in the more censorious 1980s. But TV and satire had moved on by then, helped by the outrageous *Spitting Image* puppets, who brought a new kind of irreverent send-up of politics and royalty in the late 1980s. In a sense, the puppets paved the way for the 'real thing': desperado Edina and her mad sidekick Patsy, brilliantly drawn parodies of a 1960s generation of women who saw themselves as fully paid-up members of the 'have it all' society with sex, money, booze, drugs, fashion, fads and celebrity all exploding onto the screen and letting rip as never before.

Right from the sound of the opening notes of the wonderful theme tune, 'This Wheel's on Fire' (written by Bob

Dylan in the 1960s and re-recorded by Julie Driscoll and Ade especially for *Ab Fab*), to the initial sighting of Edina and co., that very first episode of *Ab Fab* in November 1992 meant one thing: the time had come to celebrate – and laugh non-stop – at the sight of women behaving really badly.

Relentless, frenetic over-the-top behaviour, Jennifer Saunders-style, was about to launch itself into the national psyche. And there would be plenty more of this type of mayhem to come...

CHAPTER 4

MORE BOLLY, SWEETIE

They laughed until the tears came. Day in, day out, their laughter echoed around the rehearsal room as they improvised the scenes, brought the characters to life. An ageing PR woman, a nympho ex-model, a grandmother, a strait-laced 20-something and a hopeless PA locked in a cynical, upside-down world of designer fashion, fads and freebies, stumbling around, living it large, ridiculous and a tad shocking in their excess.

Then, when the hour came, the women of *Ab Fab* stepped out and did it all over again. But this time they performed in front of a studio audience – and the crowd lapped up every minute, every time. Gales of laughter out front, one very happy band of performers. It worked, didn't it?

How could it not work? Right from the very first episode when PR Edina organises a historic fashion show – 'I'm going to go down in history, Pats, as the woman that put Princess Anne into a Vivienne Westwood basque' – the outrageous adventures of the *Ab Fab* cast were bound to create a smash hit and keep audiences doubled up with laughter for decades.

This was the dysfunctional *Ab Fab* 'family' seen on BBC2 in November 1992 when the debut episode went out: Edina ('Eddy') Monsoon (Jennifer) is a middle-aged, twice-divorced mess of a woman, with two children by different fathers, running a PR business at which she rarely works – and when she does, it's a disaster. A child of the 1960s, Edina refuses to grow up. She's rude, a fashion victim in outrageously gaudy and expensive designer gear from Christian Lacroix, Pucci – you name it, she wears it, even if it is too small. A messy, loud woman making a spectacle of herself wherever she lands. She spends her time chasing bizarre fads and fashionable causes in an attempt to stay hip and youthful: New Age, Greenpeace, Buddhism, colonic irrigation, fad diets that never seem to work.

Her best friend Patsy Stone (Joanna Lumley) is even more over the top: a fashion director for a glossy magazine with a permanent hangover, she does so little work she's forgotten where her office is (she only got the job because she slept with the publisher). Taller, slimmer, blonder than Edina, with an Ivana Trump-style hairdo and a habitual fag dangling from her lips, Patsy is the ultimate sponger with the morals of an alley cat. Dressed mostly in Betty Jackson, Chanel or Jasper Conran, she lives on a diet of cigarettes, drink, drugs and younger men.

Work for these two women is one long lunch break at a

fashionable restaurant, shopping at Harvey Nichols or a night's clubbing.

Watching over the proceedings with horror from Edina's expensive three-storey house in west London is her young daughter, Saffron (Julia Sawalha), the only normal person in the household (Edina's son, Serge, initially is away at university). As virtuous and straight as Edina and Patsy are unhinged, 'Saffy' is usually required to play the parent to the pair's excesses – 'You're no better than a junkie,' She tells Eddy at one point. Saffy is far too sensible to be corrupted by her mother. She's a plain Jane who prefers science to sex and books to booze.

Edina's own mother (June Whitfield) remains the butt of her daughter's loathing – however, she's something of a kleptomaniac and not at all scared of speaking her mind. And backing up the quartet is a brainless, blithely ignorant but chirpy PA, appropriately named Bubble (Jane Horrocks).

Interestingly enough, Horrocks originally auditioned for the part of Saffron, but, seeing her comic talent, Jennifer adapted the role of Bubble for her.

So where did these larger-than-life characters and their world spring from?

Essentially, *Ab Fab* was a mirror of its age. Its characters had spent the 1980s living off other people's talents but by the 1990s could not quite accept that the party had either come to an abrupt end – or had moved on without them. The *Ab Fab* world was made up of a mostly freeloading, hedonistic crowd – hangers-on in the London fashion, showbiz, music and pop worlds, who had made their way onto the guest list for PR bashes and first nights at some point yet continued to lead the same somewhat pointless 'freebie' life, despite the onset of middle age.

'They could go on *Mastermind* and answer questions about Harvey Nichols,' Jennifer told the *Daily Telegraph* in 1992. 'But they'd never know what anything cost. The fashion and music businesses are full of them and I suppose they do no real harm. Their worst crime is thinking that what they do is important.'

So where did Edina come from?

'Edina came from the story that your wildest friends bring up the straightest kids,' Jennifer revealed to *Tatler* magazine in 1992. 'And from a story of a friend's mother who wore turbans and was always big and wonderful, and would stand starkers on her veranda in her villa in Greece, shouting: "I am Aphrodite."'

'People might be offended by this show and if they are, then I'm sorry,' she continued. 'But that's not why it's there. I just think it's funny, I can't help it.'

As for Patsy, Jennifer credits Joanna Lumley with her creation.

'Joanna invented Patsy in a way,' she told Sue Lawley on *Desert Island Discs* in 1996. 'I wrote the lines, but the character came from her.'

Jennifer's beady-eyed observation of the social mores of the hedonistic early 1990s in London clearly played a huge part in the creation of *Ab Fab* as a parody of real life. Add to that the use of improvisation, letting situations evolve and characters come to life in rehearsal rather than following a set script, plotted out word by word, and you have the real key to its wickedly entertaining appeal.

With that kind of freedom, the hilariously funny characters emerged in those early rehearsals, rather than springing fully formed off the scripted page. In fact, filming the initial pilot show was, for Jennifer, the important creative tipping point.

'Once I saw people on the screen like Joanna Lumley brilliantly bringing her part alive, I was then writing for real characters, not just writing a monologue.'

Incredibly, Joanna very nearly didn't take the role that revived her career and turned her into an international star at the age of 46. The former 1960s model, Bond girl and star of *The Avengers* had met Ruby Wax for the first time backstage at a West End theatre where Joanna had been working in a play called *Vanilla* – which had bombed. Ruby, spotting Joanna's hitherto untested comic potential, insisted that she should guest on her TV show, *The Full Wax* and told Joanna she should be working with *French and Saunders*. (Following their *Girls on Top* collaboration, Jennifer had made brief guest appearances alongside Ruby in *The Full Wax* in 1991 and 1992; Ruby continued to work with her as a script editor after that time.)

In due course, Joanna received a script for the pilot of *Ab Fab* – and loved it. But as she recalled in her book, *Absolutely*, when she turned up to meet Jennifer for the first time to give a read-through for Patsy, she couldn't seem to 'get' the character of Patsy at all.

She had no idea at all what Patsy was supposed to be like. All she knew was that Patsy was 'a friend'.

'I couldn't seem to make her sound like the person she was hoping for,' recalled Joanna in her memoir, *Absolutely*. She went home, rang her agent and said, 'Get me out of this.'

'Oh come on,' said her agent. 'It's only a pilot, it may never get made, and anyway, you are skint.'

'All I can remember is inventing (for myself) a person, largely based on a cartoon version of me, who had her own life and history and a way of walking with a hunched back and a sneery voice, and trying it out in scenes with Jennifer,' said Joanna in *Absolutely*.

Once she had got Jennifer to laugh, she carried on with more of the same.

'Jennifer had opened a Pandora's box for me with her outrageously inventive writing,' she recalled in *Absolutely*.

'We invented Patsy's past and I furnished her with having been a model in the Swinging Sixties,' Joanna told the *Guardian* in 2011. 'Jennifer is 13 years younger than me, so she was a baby when all that was going on. But she's like a Hoover, she's like a scavenger. She's a bottom-of-the-pond feeder. She goes around listening and picking anything she wants from anywhere. She's a wizard.'

That first series of *Absolutely Fabulous* was a big success: it attracted an audience of 8 million. Jennifer, with typical modesty, said afterwards: 'I don't take it seriously. In my head, I know how clever *Ab Fab* is – and it's not that clever. A lot is panic combined with a nice atmosphere and a brilliant cast and director [Bob Spiers]. But it's only a sitcom. Television is trivial, which is why I love it.

'I was surprised by its success. I thought it would get by and hopefully no one would notice. I realised I'd get slagged off for the drinking, drugs and overacting. I hate that Puritan attitude. There's so much really wrong in the world, we should be allowed to act badly, park on the pavement occasionally and just live.

'I think that is exactly why I go so much over the top in *Ab Fab* because I think: "There! I've done it now! All right? Is that all right? And I have to make it bigger and bigger and neurotic, *very* neurotic and drunk, drunk, oh please yes, drunk."

'I think people would like to live like Edina and Patsy. We're quite strict with ourselves nowadays; I think people would have more pleasure if they lived like them.'

The amazing success of that first series of *Ab Fab* was further fuelled by newspaper headlines claiming that Jennifer had, in fact, based Edina on a real-life public relations person Lynne Franks.

Jennifer denied this claim, although the two women already knew each other. Throughout the late 1980s, Franks had been running one of the most high-profile and successful fashion PR companies in the UK, with clients that included Jean Paul Gaultier, Jasper Conran and Katharine Hamnett. Well known for her parties, her power, her love of Buddhism and chanting and her outlandish outfits (try a dirndl skirt, orange and purple ankle socks and purple hair for a visit to New York's Studio 54) around the time *Ab Fab* came out Franks had divorced her husband, quit the PR business and moved to LA. Yet the similarities between her frenetic public relations world and that of Eddy were impossible to ignore. And the newspapers, many of whose writers knew Franks, enjoyed ramping up the whole story.

At one point, there were reports that Jennifer got the idea for *Ab Fab* after holidaying with Lynne at Franks' villa in Deya, Mallorca, but it was never quite clear just how much of Eddy had been derived from the real life and times of Lynne Franks.

Today, Lynne Franks is a women's empowerment guru and co-founder of B.Hive, a chain of women's business clubs.

'I was friends with Jennifer and Dawn and doing their PR for a period of time,' she recalled. 'Through working with them, I introduced them to the fashion world, some designers, fashion people. In 1989, I organised for them to present an award at the very first British Fashion Awards. So they went backstage afterwards and met various fashion people.

'And then, because they were clients of mine – as were Lenny Henry and Ruby Wax then – they'd come to my office parties – and they'd see all the PR world in action.

'Jennifer never stayed with me in Mallorca. We were good friends and we had been on holiday together: Dawn and Jennifer used to turn up at my house and do their *French and Saunders* thing, chanting and joking around. We had wonderful times together. Then I didn't see them for a while because we were not representing them for periods of time. When they had things to push, we'd represent them but when we weren't working with them, we'd occasionally meet up for lunch, as friends do.

'I heard that the *Ab Fab* series was starting because Janet Street-Porter told me – she was working at the Beeb at the time. But I didn't know the details. I was invited to come and watch the recordings of the show and even invited to go on the show – which I turned down – but after they'd started recording it, then I heard what it was all about from various people.

'I didn't know enough about it but I did meet Jennifer at a party. And she said it was not based on me.'

Franks now wishes she hadn't been quite so huffy about all the headlines and the 'Is this the real-life Edina?' stories at the time.

'It was really a thing that was built up by the media. Then it started to get more annoying because it was always brought up in interviews with the press.

'I thought the show was brilliant. I loved it. The only thing that upset me were the scenes where Eddy and Saffy were falling out – I thought people might believe this was based on me and my daughter.'

The similarities between Eddy's world and hers were, she admits, quite apparent. The *Ab Fab* house was similar to hers, as was the kitchen – there were recognisable things from her life. And she had talked to Jennifer about Buddhism and tree hugging.

'But that's what writers do, they collect material all the time.'

Franks says the problem was that her own life had undergone dramatic changes when the series came out.

'I had actually sold my business by this time – at the suggestion of my ex-husband – which I now regret. But selling my business had nothing to do with anything around the show. It was a strange experience to be going through a huge life change at the time the series was on. But that's just the way it was.'

Today, she regrets not appearing in the show.

'And I also regret that I didn't take it more with a bit of humour. I should have been a lot lighter about it.'

Nonetheless, she says she is flattered to be part of such a phenomenally successful show that has continued to be popular down the years.

'*Ab Fab* was a women's project, created by women and loved by women – and gay men. And it's important for all women everywhere to be able to laugh at themselves.

'If someone bases a sitcom on you, you've got to have a sense of humour about it all.'

Julia Sawalha recalled that right from the moment when the *Ab Fab* cast started working on the show there was a distinct freedom for the actors in its women-behaving-badly or 'ladette' sensibility: 'It showed that women were capable of being smutty and drinking too much, and it was such a relief to see that. It's important to be able to take the piss out of yourself and Jennifer is so good at that.'

But how did Dawn feel about Jennifer's huge solo success?

She had made a brief appearance in the final episode of the first *Ab Fab* series in December 1992. And by then, of course, the duo had started working together again, creating the fourth series of *French and Saunders* – in the same office at the BBC where Jennifer had worked on *Ab Fab*.

'I don't think she's jealous of its success,' said Jennifer at the time. 'She hates awards or anything like that. The show's been so hyped since it's been on, I don't even recognise what people say about it anymore,' she added.

Dawn, as usual, used humour to sidestep the issue: 'You feel a kind of pride as well as utter fury and jealousy, but that's what makes you do your own work better. We are competitive, but it's a sort of friendly competitive. It's like being jealous of a friend who looks great, but you still love her.'

But if their close relationship – described by showbiz insiders as 'a kind of marriage' – proved stronger than any competitive feelings, getting down to creating a fourth series of *French and Saunders* was still a big challenge. Any kind of success sets the bar just as high, if not higher.

'You could say we've been working on it for the past two years, because we've been scribbling down ideas for at least that long. The problem is not so much thinking of funny sketches but thinking of new ways to do them. For instance, we decided we had done enough parody in the other series, and that this time there'd be no parody. I'd say it's about 40 per cent parody and rising now,' she told the *Daily Telegraph* in 1992.

The fourth series of six *French and Saunders'* episodes was screened in February 1993 on BBC2. And yes, it was mostly parody – of the hilarious kind. Hollywood movies such as *Misery*, *Silence of the Lambs* (a memorable skit with Dawn as Hannibal Lecter) and *Thelma & Louise* were sent up mercilessly and there was an entertaining spoof of the hit BBC costume drama of the early 1990s, *The House of Eliott* (renamed 'The House of Idiot'), with Kathy Burke and *House of Eliott* star, Louise Lombard.

Whatever the career hurdles they had overcome, at home in leafy Richmond, family life with Ade and her three daughters remained, as always, Jennifer's solidly grounding anchor. There was a lot of juggling of schedules – ideally, one partner would take over or be around at home if the other was away working or in the studio filming. It took a lot of planning.

'It's a matter of becoming more organised. Children force you to organise your life and sort yourself out a bit,' said Jennifer. 'It's not like I have a nine-to-five job, these are the people I feel sorry for.

'I hope I'm a good mother, but I don't follow a plan or reason with them. They have to grow up to realise just how bad things can be. If they do something wrong and I'm in a bad mood, I shout. I won't bargain. They look at me and go: "Leave her, she's tired."'

She probably wasn't joking. With two TV series coming to life in just under a year – the second, much-anticipated series of *Ab Fab* on BBC1 was scheduled for January 1994 – there wasn't much time for quiet relaxation. The pressure was on.

In April 1993, Jennifer and Dawn had teamed up again with The Comic Strip gang in a 30-minute *Comic Strip Presents* film, *Space Virgins from Planet Sex*, in which the girls played sex-mad aliens in a James Bond-type spoof created by Peter Richardson, shown on BBC2.

One month later, the BBC made a major announcement: the joint comic talents of Jennifer and Dawn were far too valuable to take for granted. Determined to limit all competition from ITV and Channel 4, they signed the pair up on an exclusive, ground-breaking five-year contract, reputed then to be worth £2 million.

At the time, this was quite extraordinary: the longest contract the BBC had ever signed with an entertainment act (in today's terms, such a deal would be worth around £4 million to £5 million).

The deal prevented the pair from working for any other British TV station, but it gave them both freedom, as a double act and in their own right, to work on separate projects, so long as they produced an average of two of their own comedy series each year. In a sense, it meant they were 'married' to the BBC, but it was an 'open' marriage: if they wished, they could also work on other projects.

Alan Yentob was Controller of BBC1 at the time. He announced the contract at the Golden Rose TV Festival in Montreux, Switzerland. Yentob had always been a champion of Jennifer and Dawn when he was Controller of BBC2, describing them as a 'particularly rare breed of entertainment'.

It was another accolade for French and Saunders as comic performers. No other comedy duo since the days of Morecambe & Wise had captured public affection and large audiences in quite the same way. And now they both had other successful series as extra strings to their bows: Jennifer with *Ab Fab* and Dawn with *Murder Most Horrid*.

Jennifer was swift to play down the news of their signing the 'golden handcuffs' deal.

'We're not given a sum of money. We just get paid for the actual number of programmes we produce,' she admitted to *The Sunday Times*.

'We might end up with a million if we worked every hour of every day for five years, but that's not going to happen,' she told the *Sunday Express*.

Jennifer has frequently claimed that she is very far from a workaholic.

'I like having fun. I'm not ambitious,' she recalled. Ambition, she believed, could ruin lives.

'You become miserable. We've had jealousy from comedians who think we've sold out instead of doing the comedy circuit. That suits me fine. You reach a time when you don't want to do anything frightening.'

'Dawn and I are something of a showbiz rarity in that we have managed to maintain a successful double act and remain close friends,' Jennifer told *TV Times* magazine in March 1990. 'The act exists as a result of the friendship; we work together because we enjoy it. No fun, no act, that's our motto. And Dawn is a great motivator, which proves a useful asset in our relationship. She is a great doer.'

Tim Anderson has been a Fleet Street freelance photographer for over two decades, photographing royals and celebrities for newspapers and magazines. He has photographed Jennifer on a number of occasions, mainly during the early *Ab Fab* years when he sometimes worked as a unit stills photographer on the set at the BBC studios while *Ab Fab* was being filmed.

Anderson was sent to photograph Dawn and Jennifer for a national newspaper interview just after the new contract with the BBC had been announced. As he remembers it, this was a somewhat apprehensive situation.

'We were warned beforehand they might say they don't want to do any pictures. Which is a bit strange. But once it was underway, it was fine. But that kind of reluctance is very unusual for anyone, particularly for someone playing such an outgoing character.'

Anderson's overall impression? 'She is an introvert, very very quiet. Polite but nothing at all like the characters she plays. Which is quite common with some very funny people. She does literally turn it on when she performs, especially with Edina in *Ab Fab*. – she really is an alter ego.

'When you're doing unit stills, you actually shoot while they're filming the show. But because they have to film from different angles and stop briefly, the stills photographer on the set gets a bit of downtime. So you can sometimes do some quick shots of a performer if they're OK with that.

'Jennifer was fine with that sort of thing – as Edina. She's far more gregarious and approachable while she's in character. Otherwise she's quiet. Not at all what you would expect.'

Jennifer herself has admitted that playing such an outrageously extrovert character in *Ab Fab* and 'acting out' all the time on set did leave some kind of imprint on her everyday personality from time to time: 'Ade says that when I come back from *Ab Fab* recordings my arrogance level has gone up. It's to be expected. All the decisions [on the show] come back to me and I have to be dominant, so I come home still on a high.'

And what a high it was. That summer, extracts for the second series of *Ab Fab* were shot on location in the desert in Morocco (subsequent series extracts were to take the *Ab Fab* team to New York, the South of France and Paris, though the complete show was always recorded live before a studio audience). The second series also included a glittering array of celebrities, including Helena Bonham Carter, Richard E. Grant, Suzi Quatro, Mandy Rice-Davies, Britt Ekland, Lulu, Jo Brand, Zandra Rhodes, Meera Syal and Miranda Richardson.

'It is worse to get real people to try and pretend they're celebrities, that looks dreadful,' said Jennifer. 'It's better to get the real thing. Edina moves in those kind of circles – they're not gratuitously there.'

Yet given the overwhelming success of the first series of *Ab Fab*, Jennifer was well aware of the pressure to maintain the momentum and the growing expectation around her further attempts to portray Britain's most erratic and dysfunctional comic family.

At the Edinburgh Festival in August 1993 she even talked of her intention to end *Ab Fab* at some point, saying that she wanted it to be remembered as 'absolutely brilliant' before it ran out of steam.

'You have to think whether you can keep coming up with fresh ideas,' she told the festival audience. 'If there is the slightest danger you can't, you shouldn't risk carrying on.'

At the end of 1993, *Absolutely Fabulous* had scooped a brace of industry awards: Writers' Guild of Great Britain Award for Jennifer (for TV Situation Comedy), two British Comedy Awards for Joanna Lumley (Best Comedy Actress and Top TV Personality), a British Comedy Award for Best New Comedy for *Ab Fab*, and a BAFTA for Best Comedy Series for *Ab Fab* which went to Jennifer, producer Jon Plowman and the director, the late Bob Spiers. To cap this, *Ab Fab* also won an International Emmy Award in New York that November.

For *French and Saunders*, Jennifer and Dawn were also awarded a British Comedy Award for Top Female Performers. (This particular Comedy Awards night catapulted the awards into showbiz legend, when comic entertainer Julian Clary's lewd remarks about the then Chancellor of the Exchequer, Norman Lamont, caused media outrage – and very nearly derailed Clary's career for good.)

But there was no time to sit back and contemplate their respective navels. That autumn, Jennifer and Dawn were given the opportunity to go for another first – their first ever appearance together in a West End play – as actors, in someone else's material. It was a step in an unusual direction for the duo, but it meant a fresh challenge and so they decided to go for it.

The play, *Me and Mamie O'Rourke*, opened in London's Strand Theatre in December 1993 and ran until April 1994. Written by Mary Agnes Donoghue (best known as the writer of the Hollywood weepie *Beaches*, starring Bette Midler), in many ways it was an ideal vehicle for the two women.

Set in a somewhat claustrophobic basement, it's a story of female friendship, focusing on two close friends: Louise (Jennifer), whose architect husband is wrecking the rest of the house as he converts it (a metaphor for the couple's disintegrating marriage), and her divorced friend Bibi, a cook who dreams of being an animal behaviourist (Dawn).

The two women escape the realities of their world, with fantasy scenarios, a world of their own, which deflects from the unhappiness of their lives. Two close friends creating other worlds for themselves: strong echoes of French and Saunders' working relationship?

'I suppose it does echo our writing process,' said Jennifer during rehearsal. 'When we know we will be forced into a room for most of the day, and we plan it out, and we know it's going to be such fun, and gossipy, and I suppose we still think that that will push all the difficult stuff, all the work, out of the way.'

Mary Agnes Donoghue decided they were perfect for the roles (some of the dialogue certainly bears a striking resemblance to a *French and Saunders'* sketch). 'I didn't write it for them,' she said when the play opened, 'but suddenly you could see their style in it: it was a perfect sort of match.'

Much press attention was given to the fact that the play contains a scene where the two women kiss.

'It's not really a snog, more of an embarrassed peck,' said Jennifer. 'They come to realise the fact that they actually have dreadful lives. There's a moment where they get completely drunk one evening and they think: "Oh well, who's the person I like best in the world?" And it's each other. So they think: "Well maybe we're gay." Then an embarrassed kiss is all they can manage.'

Yet working with someone else's material was not so easy or straightforward as they might have thought. When you normally share total control of the entire process, having someone else oversee your performance requires a certain kind of adjustment.

'What's tough is being directed, because we're used to doing what we find by instinct. I'm not really confident because I haven't done something like it before. And I have less control over it than I have had over anything for a very long time,' confessed Jennifer.

Although the play drew the crowds, the reviews were mixed. Not everyone was convinced that this was a good vehicle for the two women's respective talents.

'Their fans will be hard pressed to respond to *Mamie* with anything beyond bewilderment,' wrote *Variety*'s Matt Wolf.

'The duo make an alcohol-fuelled lesbian try-out a likeable enough clown routine, French heaving herself over Saunders in a way that suggests it would be more comfortable getting fresh with Moby Dick,' said the *Independent*'s Paul Taylor. 'Maybe this deservedly popular pair are just repressing a keen desire to send it up rotten.'

Other reviews were no kinder: 'The whole unutterably dire affair will disappoint any *French and Saunders* admirers hoping for a barrage of TV sketches or anything as good as *Absolutely Fabulous*,' said the *Observer*.

One problem that Jennifer encountered as a stage actor was her far too relaxed, laid-back approach to stagecraft. 'There was a moment when I was holding a prop, a magazine, and I actually started to read the magazine – and could just not remember where we were in the play,' she recalled.

She also found the repetitive nature of a long theatre run lasting four months difficult – 'it's not a life I'm cut out for' – and candidly revealed that if it hadn't been for her relationship with Dawn, the run could have been extra-tough for her.

'Imagine having to make friends with someone else, seeing them night after night in the dressing room, having to get into their lives. That's the drawback of a long run. Whereas with Dawn and me, that's all taken care of,' she said.

Afterwards, Dawn explained a little bit more about her friend's feelings. The play hadn't been a disaster, but it left Jennifer with a feeling that a long theatre run just wasn't right for her.

'She vowed never to return to the stage after that. It wasn't the play. It was how claustrophobic and trapped she felt,' said Dawn.

Nearly two decades later, Jennifer recollected the memory of acting in a play for a long run to BBC Radio 2 listeners. 'I'll never be in another play. It shocked me. It goes on and on every night and in that play I never came off stage, which is ridiculous.'

Earlier in 1993 she had recorded a voice-only role as the fairy in an animated children's cartoon, *Prince Cinders* (based on the Cinderella story), which went out on Channel 4 on Christmas Eve. And days later, the second series of *Ab Fab* received a warm reception when it 'moved up' from BBC2 and went out on BBC1 in January 1994, though some sniffy reviewers thought it 'a bit contrived'.

Audiences didn't care – they still loved it. The first episode, where Patsy has a secret affair with a politician, only to be rumbled by the tabloids in an ensuing sex scandal, proved to have an uncanny similarity to a real-life sex scandal. Amazingly enough, at the beginning of January, Conservative MP and Minister for the Environment Tim Yeo had been forced to resign following a scandal involving a 'love child' born to a Tory councillor.

'It's pure coincidence that the subject is so topical,' said Jennifer, pointing out that the episode had been filmed months before. 'That kind of thing never seems to be out of the news, anyway.'

She had a point. Sleaze, alas, would continue to dog the Conservative government of the time. Using topicality is, of course, an *Ab Fab* hallmark: Jennifer freely admitted that she had even used scenes from her own household as the basis for some of Patsy's more explosive moments.

'I've worked all the tantrums my kids have ever had into the show – and Patsy has them! The other day I said to Freya: "I'm going to work now, can I just have a little cuddle before I go? Can I have a little cuddle?" And she just lifted up her little toe and said: "Yes, you can cuddle my foot." I looked at her and she went: "You can cuddle my foot." She's three years old and she's a teenager.'

As for Edina Monsoon, Jennifer revealed that her behaviour at home towards her three children was far from Edina-like: 'Actually, I'm the opposite. I'm terribly strict. Ade's the nice one who's always handing out treats. I think if you have strict parents you'll probably have wild and rebellious children. I hope my girls go a bit wild – it'll be much more fun.'

For Jennifer, escaping into the world of Edina and Patsy never failed to delight.

'It's the most lovely thing. It's hard to describe but when I'm being Eddy and Joanna becomes Patsy and we're sitting there, I think there's no happier place to be because it is a total escape,' Jennifer told *The Times* in July 2005. 'It must be for us like meditation is for other people who can lose themselves through it. You become those people and you think of funnier and funnier things. And Joanna and I will sit for an hour and just have a conversation about whatever Patsy might do, how they would end up, where they might have gone, what would happen if they did this or that. And it's like eating the best chocolate!

'I don't think she [Edina] is completely separate from me,' she told *The New York Times* in an interview in July 1995. 'I think I've got quite a lot of her neuroses, like anyone does. She's just a concentrated form of most people's lives. If you start to think about one thing in life that annoys you, you can exaggerate it to make it Edina's problem.'

Following the International Emmy Award, there was a great deal of interest from US TV companies wanting to do their own TV version of *Ab Fab*. In mid-1994, it was announced that the US cable channel Comedy Central would be airing the series and, in July, the niche American TV channel aired all 12 episodes in one weekend's screening, repeating it constantly.

That first weekend's screening on Comedy Central netted around 800,000 viewers – a record for the network (which was just three years old at the time) but a relatively small audience for the US. There were reports from Comedy Central that at the Hollywood preview 'they went gaga', according to the cable channel's spokesman. 'People are talking about it left and right,' he said. And it wasn't long before the US critics joined in the praise.

For *USA Today*, Patsy was 'a tour de force creation of blistering attitude'. And Jennifer's performance was 'an absolute riot, a berserk and blowsy fashion publicist forever in a groggy hangover'.

The 'heat' around *Absolutely Fabulous* was now a major preoccupation for American TV executives. In December 1994, Jennifer jetted to Los Angeles for face-to-face meetings with US film and TV executives who were eager to meet the creator of the series that was causing such a stir.

At the same time, actor Richard E. Grant was on a promotional tour for the movie *Prêt-à-Porter* ('ready to wear'), an insider's look at the fashion industry in which he starred as a fashion designer, Cort Romney – 'a male Vivienne Westwood'. Directed by Robert Altman, the high-profile movie starred a number of European and American actors, including Julia Roberts, Sophia Loren, Rupert Everett and Kim Basinger. Grant was joined by Jennifer as the Brit contingent took part in the glittering brouhaha surrounding the movie's LA premiere.

'Rupert Everett, Rossy de Palma and I wait for Jennifer Saunders to arrive,' wrote Grant in his Los Angeles diary. 'She's my date as my wife has gone home.

'Having taken meetings from every top honcho in town (including Mr Spielberg) for *Absolutely Fabulous*, she amazes us with tales of Hollywood's highest humbling themselves at her feet.

'When people see Ms Saunders they introduce themselves in a torrential gust of "Oh my Gaaaad! It really is *Absolutely Fabulous*." Jennifer provides a running commentary, her verbal doodlebugs detonating just short of the target as they approach and gush. Which they do like so many overdressed oil rigs, all night long.'

It had been a very busy year. Jennifer's hectic schedule had involved filming again in North Africa earlier in 1994. Only this time, it wasn't for an outrageous *Ab Fab* location scene but for the leading role in a one-hour BBC drama, based on a trio of real-life stories called *Heroes and Villains*. Jennifer's episode, 'Queen of the East', told the story of Lady Hester Stanhope, an eccentric aristocrat in Victorian times and also an ancestor of Viscountess Linley, Serena Stanhope.

As Lady Hester, Jennifer played a privileged, adventurous and statuesque woman who often dressed as a man, smoked a pipe and, according to legend, killed men with her bare hands. At 33, Lady Hester was a widow whose marriage had never been consummated. On her travels to the Middle East she met a wealthy, much younger man, who became her first lover – only to despatch him back to Europe some time later. Bloodthirsty and with delusions of grandeur, Lady Hester declared herself the ruler of a walled city in Syria, where she died, in poverty, in 1839.

As a straight dramatic role 'Queen of the East' was a complete TV departure for Jennifer and therefore another challenge. And it was a tough shoot – several weeks in the intense heat and scorching sun of the North African desert.

'Lady Hester was a true maverick and it needed a strong actress to take on her memory. Jennifer is brilliant – we couldn't have found better,' said producer Greg Brenman.

The programme went out on BBC1 on 26 January 1995. It was not very well received by the critics, partly because there was so much comic potential in the sight of an imperious Jennifer on horseback, in flowing robes, making her way through the desert. Visually, it could easily have been a movie spoof from *French and Saunders* or *Ab Fab* – and so the critics sharpened their claws ('Arab Fab' was one of the politer descriptions).

'Whatever Lady Hester Stanhope was really like, it's a safe bet that she was strikingly dissimilar to the overbearing, self-deluding proto-Thatcherite gargoyle hilariously impersonated by Saunders,' said the *Independent*. 'Her increasing sense of destiny was matched, frame for frame, by a corresponding growth in absurdity.'

The clunky dialogue didn't help. 'Sometimes I want to take all my clothes off,' said the younger lover to Lady Hester – before taking all his clothes off.

'A remark by Hester's increasingly rebellious lover – "We make it all up as we go along" – rang rather truer than intended,' noted the *Guardian*.

In the spring of 1995, during the Comic Relief Red Nose Day telethon, Jennifer and Dawn appeared in what would turn out to be yet another memorable sketch: viewers were asked to pledge their money during the girls' skit with the promise that if a million pounds were raised, Dawn and a youthful Hugh Grant would exchange a passionate kiss.

The money came rolling in. And Dawn, wearing a version of Liz Hurley's famous 'safety pin' dress worn at the premiere of *Four Weddings and a Funeral*, snogged Hugh with great passion and at some length on a lip-shaped sofa – all for a million pounds.

The third series of *Ab Fab* went out in March 1995. It started off with Patsy and Edina jetting off to New York on Concorde – to buy a door handle. In the following episodes,

Lulu and Naomi Campbell made guest appearances and Patsy received a surprise visit from her sister Jackie (Kate O'Mara), who popped off to the loo every minute and munched endlessly on the potpourri, eventually forcing Edina to forgo her plans to celebrate New Year's Eve in London's trendiest nightclub. (Instead, she was forced to spend it in the bosom of her family.) Audiences and critics alike loved it.

'Jennifer Saunders proved that she can get laughs with her acting alone,' said the *Independent*'s Thomas Sutcliffe. '"I am now being taken into the sitting room to watch the New Year in on television," she announced in tones of unbridled horror; the weight of curdled loathing she gave to the site of this humiliation was worthy of Edith Evans.'

Jennifer's plan to end *Ab Fab* for good at this point seems clear from what was up on the screen: the third series ends with a fast-forward scene of Patsy and Edina some 25 years on.

Yet despite her statements about ending the series, once the show started making waves internationally it was going to be very difficult to relinquish it completely. With the two hedonists' antics deeply embedded in the psyche of their ever-growing audience, how could they suddenly vanish? Jennifer's rationale that you should quit while you're still ahead has a sound basis – and it was a valid perspective for 1980s television. But times had now changed. The sheer pulling power of *Ab Fab* around the world meant that no one else was happy to let them fade away forever.

On the home front, with their daughters now nine, eight and four, the Edmondsons continued to live a mostly normal life, carefully planning their working commitments around the girls' school holidays, so they'd have plenty of time together. It might have been easier to send them away to boarding school, but that was definitely not part of the equation.

'We're not interested in getting them ready for their O-levels at the age of six,' said Ade. 'We want them to learn how to read and write, how to be sociable and talk to people and to have the happiest time they can. Both Jennifer and I have a fairly jaundiced opinion of academic excellence. We feel we've educated ourselves more in the past 10 years than in all our time in formal education.'

At this point, with several different projects on his agenda, including two novels and a new live show of *Bottom* that year, it was difficult for anyone to equate the once-deranged, bestudded punk Vyvyan with the contented paterfamilias that Ade presented as the couple celebrated their tenth wedding anniversary. Journalists did the best they could to make much of the fact that Jennifer's star now outshone her husband's, but Ade wasn't having any of it.

'Jennifer is exceptional. A lot of people imagine she is a lot more high powered and ambitious than she is,' he told the *Daily Mail* in 1995.

'She's such a clear thinker and I don't think it's that she's particularly confident – it just seems to come naturally,' he told the *Sunday Mirror* in an interview in that same year. 'We are very different in our approaches to work. We share a two-roomed office just down the road from our house in Richmond and mine is deliberately empty of distractions – it just has my textbooks and my Oxford English Dictionary on

CD-ROM. Jennifer's is much more arranged, with posters of Marc Bolan and piles of magazines.'

Ade revealed in the same interview that he was thrilled to have a third daughter. 'I just think there are very few nice little boys. Whereas most little girls are nice. I'm turning into a real father of daughters and I'll get a shotgun licence to stand at the door to keep the boys away.'

The couple, always keen to retreat to the rural life, away from the glare of publicity and the demands of showbiz, had bought a place in Devon at the beginning of 1995. If work commitments permitted, the Edmondsons could spend the entire summer there – and Jennifer and the girls could go horse riding.

'We're not competitive,' Ade revealed. 'Our work is part of our normal life, being married. If your marriage has sunk to the depths of professional jealousy – which could happen to a librarian and a professor of physics, or anyone – you're in a sad way.'

Their comic acting roles as rebel punk married to flamboyant fashion victim might have fixed them in the public consciousness as two over-the-top individuals, but in reality, life chez Edmondson remained remarkably settled and calm.

'The eldest is so far from being rebellious, it's frightening,' revealed Ade. 'She's incredibly obedient of authority and worries if we park where we shouldn't or haven't got a seat belt on. She'll tell Jennifer off for smoking and keeps us all in line.

'We don't let them watch what we do on television because I think they are too young for most of it.'

December 1995 saw the UK opening of *In the Bleak Midwinter*, also known as *A Midwinter's Tale*, written and directed by Kenneth Branagh. The film, in which Jennifer played a cameo role as Nancy Crawford, a Hollywood movie executive, tells the story of Joe Harper, an out-of-work actor (Michael Maloney), who puts on a Christmas production of *Hamlet* in a country church, a subtly comic tale of actors and their foibles.

Shot in black and white in London in just three weeks and starring Joan Collins as Joe's cynical theatrical agent, Margaretta D'Arcy, with a cast that included Richard Briers, Celia Imrie, John Sessions and Julia Sawalha, the movie (known as *A Midwinter's Tale* in the US) won two awards for Kenneth Branagh, at the 1995 Boston Film Festival and at the 1995 Venice Film Festival.

'I enjoyed having Joan Collins grovelling to me but in other respects I found the film quite terrifying because it's very much an ensemble piece in which all the rest of the cast knew each other well and I came in late in the day to do a small part – and with a Texan accent,' said Jennifer afterwards.

Jennifer's cameo did not please everyone. 'As a Hollywood producer, Jennifer Saunders delivers the sort of patronising caricature that one associates with the British cinema of 40 years ago,' pronounced veteran movie critic Philip French.

Maybe this was just one Hollywood send-up too far for Saunders. Or maybe, as she hinted, it was all a bit too rushed: after all, she'd now had personal experience of Hollywood types.

It is tempting to speculate that all those gushing 'hellos' in LA for *Ab Fab*, as described by Richard E. Grant, would have given her sharp observer's eye an even harsher picture, close up, of how the fame game works in Hollywood or US television, where an overnight smash hit becomes a failure if the next project bombs and the most gushing devotees can abruptly cease to acknowledge your existence. And anyway, sending up or lampooning showbiz and its habits was already an established part of her repertoire.

Who can blame Jennifer for not being pitch perfect just this once?

CHAPTER 5

40-SOMETHING

*A*bsolutely *Fabulous* had struck another Holy Grail of British TV programme makers: the chance to reach a massive audience in the US. And while it started out there with a cult following, over time the show turned out to be a huge hit internationally. It was also an instant success with the gay community, following the US cable launch on Comedy Central.

'The show's influence on pop culture, particularly in gay male circles, is all-pervasive,' said the US gay and lesbian news magazine, *The Advocate*.

'Sociologists will easily pinpoint the mid-1990s as the time when the campy [phrase] "girlfriend" was supplanted by the camper "sweetie, darling".'

Eventually, other gay communities around the world also fell heavily for the charms of Edina and Patsy. Why, you wonder, did the show make this impact with the gay world?

'The gay community is usually the first to jump onto what is smart and new – and the characters are quite easy to imitate,' said Joanna Lumley.

'Edina would love to hang around with gay people; it's more interesting,' added Jennifer. 'Our gay audience is fantastic. I hope we're so popular with gay people because we're a bit different. And maybe it's because we don't give a shit. Dawn and I are obviously gay men in disguise: look at the people we've had on the show or we've impersonated. We're totally in love with all gay icons.'

Rupert Mellor has been a film and showbiz journalist for 20 years. He believes the gay world fell so completely for Edina and Patsy because the drag queen – the heavily made-up, garishly attired, male in female guise – is so much a part of gay culture.

'What *Ab Fab* did was give us the ultimate, utterly modern, completely savvy drag queen, interpreted by women. And because they are women, it brought in the whole diva thing, the diva power that always fascinates gay men – these strong women, in a world that is set against them, defiantly doing their own thing.

'And the fact that they are spoilt and narcissistic has connections with the gay psyche. As well as gay people's ability to laugh at themselves.

'It's not that gays want to be Edina and Patsy. They want to be their friends. The girls are the ultimate fag hags: fun, shamelessly self-indulgent and insanely overdressed. And what is also important is that they are really loyal friends, despite the daftness. They are their own tribe.'

But despite their success, the mainstream American TV networks of the mid-1990s were not quite ready for the antics of Patsy and Edina. (In those early days on Comedy Central, some four-letter words were bleeped out or drowned by the sound of audience applause.)

Roseanne Barr had a huge US smash hit in the late 1980s with her ABC TV blue-collar family sitcom *Roseanne*, seen in the UK on Channel 4. She was also the closest loud-mouthed, over-the-top female comic character to Edina on American TV at that time.

Roseanne loved the *Ab Fab* concept. And she was one of the many US film and television people who approached Jennifer to buy the American rights to the series.

In January 1995, the American rights to *Ab Fab* were sold to Roseanne for a reported £250,000, following many meetings with Hollywood figures and their entourages during Jennifer's December LA trip. (It was also reported at the time that Roseanne impressed Jennifer because she was the only one to turn up for meetings without any hangers-on.)

There were also reports that Jennifer had signed a deal to write a screenplay for an *Absolutely Fabulous* movie, to be made in the UK – a project that would frequently be talked about but would wax and wane over the years ahead.

Roseanne, not surprisingly, wanted to make her own version of the show for the US market. She even wrote a script for the US version. Big names such as Carrie Fisher and Barbara Carrera were mooted to play the Patsy and

Edina characters – but nothing came of it. Roseanne couldn't interest any of the major US television networks in her version of *Ab Fab*. (Legend has it that even Steven Spielberg tried – and failed – to convince the major networks to take the show.)

Why wouldn't they take *Ab Fab*? In the simplest terms, it was just too racy for the big US networks with their huge audiences. Essentially, the sight of women behaving badly, falling around dead drunk, taking drugs and smoking, was something the major networks would not contemplate showing to their massive audiences, given the power of their sponsors, the advertisers.

Initially this came as a bit of a shock to Jennifer, who regarded *Ab Fab* as essentially an extension of the work she and Dawn had been doing for years with *French and Saunders* – two lazy women acting like children, the perfect double-act concept.

'In England, it was: "Oh, bloody drunk birds, there you go." But in America it was as if some kind of revolution had taken place. American women were going "Ohmygad! These women are so cray-zee!"' she told Ginny Dougary in an interview with *The Times* in 2005. 'And I was like "*What*? You mean you don't know anyone like that? You've never been like this yourself? You've never got drunk and fallen in the street? I don't understand: where have you been?"'

There were other subtle cultural differences, too, despite the 'special relationship' between Britain and her cousins across the pond.

'In America, you have to be seen to suffer for your deeds,'

explained Jennifer. 'So if they're going to the Betty Ford Clinic, in England we'd say: "Well, they're really going to Bermuda." But in America, they'd have to go to the Betty Ford Clinic.'

Yet Roseanne and Jennifer became quite chummy. At one point, Roseanne introduced Jennifer to Dolly Parton in Morton's, the LA celebrity hang-out of the era. It was a prize moment for Jennifer, a keen country and western fan who had always loved Dolly Parton's work. (Her other big showbiz heroine, whom she has cited as a big influence, was American TV star of the 1960s, Lucille Ball: 'Glamorous but also a clown, always making a fool of herself'.)

'She was sitting there, thin as a rake, huge tits, looking great, and I thought – in that slightly above-your-body-looking-down way – "I am sitting at a table with Dolly Parton and Roseanne Barr." And I thought: "I must not forget this moment,"' said Jennifer.

By 1996, Roseanne's sitcom needed a boost. So Patsy and Edina stepped in to perk up what was to be the final series in a guest episode, written by Jennifer, called 'Satan, Darling'.

Set at an Upper West Side party in New York, where Patsy, at one point, admits she was a man for a year – 'it dropped off' – and gulps back, with alky relish, a bottle of expensive perfume, the episode sees Edina trying her hardest to persuade Roseanne, whose sitcom character has won millions in the Lottery, to invest in DNA theme parks – creating Jackie Onassis clones for a theme park called Jackieworld – which Eddy, of course, would be paid to promote. (Never mind the fact that Patsy and Edina create mayhem while Roseanne sits behind them – in the loo.)

The *Roseanne* episode was not Jennifer's only appearance in a US production that year. She turned up briefly in Jim Henson's *Muppet Treasure Island* musical children's film based on Robert Louis Stevenson's book *Treasure Island*, one of a series of highly successful feature films featuring the Muppets, with key roles played by live-action actors.

Starring alongside the Muppets were Tim Curry, Billy Connolly, Kevin Bishop and Jennifer playing the innkeeper, Mrs Bluberidge. Released in the UK in May 1996, the film's international Muppet appeal served it well at the box office. But it really was a 'blink and you'll miss it' appearance for Jennifer's ever-growing fan base.

On the home front, the fifth series of *French and Saunders* went out on BBC1 in January 1996. And despite its high production values – the series was launched with an elaborate *Baywatch* spoof, filmed on a Somerset beach, with Dawn playing an unlikely Pamela Anderson cavorting on a 'sunny Californian' beach – and very careful – and expensive – recreations of movies such as *Batman* and *La Dolce Vita*, it failed to ignite.

Despite guests including Kate Moss, Felicity Kendal, Lulu, Lenny Henry and Julia Sawalha, the critics piled in, claiming the series relied far too heavily on Hollywood movie parodies, with sketches that went on far too long. And that the show was confusing because it was so erratic.

'Capable simultaneously of a *Batman* skit so lame it cried out for a humane killer and a beautifully observed portrayal of two mothers ramming "creative" play down the tiny gullets of their offspring, the duo no longer seem to understand just what it is they are trying to achieve,' said the *Observer*'s Ian Bell.

Reviewer Peter Hilmore was even less kind: '"Somewhere between crap and mediocre," said Kate Moss at one point in the proceedings. Unfortunately it never got near the Holy Grail of the mediocre.'

That must have hurt like hell. And it was the first time the pair had really faced such a barrage of criticism. Not surprisingly, the BBC rose to the defence of its two most successful comic performers. 'People always accuse their show of being "patchy",' said Jon Plowman, the BBC's Head of Comedy Entertainment at the time.

'Of course it is. There'll always be some things you like and some things your neighbour likes. It's in the nature of sketch shows. What Dawn and Jennifer like is exploring characters. They tend not to do quick jokes. It's not a "dash into the pub, do a joke, dash out of the pub" kind of show.'

'I don't like bad criticism. I find it quite hard to take, it makes me very cross,' admitted Jennifer afterwards. 'It's not fear of criticism, it's the anger it makes you feel, if you've had a non-constructive, bad review. Then the next thing you write you want to get back at them and show them you can do it. And that's not really a good thing.'

Yet this harsh criticism did nothing to impede the trail of success that both women had already embarked on. Dawn had a hit with *The Vicar of Dibley*, which first aired in 1994, playing the choccy-loving Reverend Geraldine Granger. The show proved to be an enormous ongoing success for her and the final series aired in 2007. And *Ab*

Fab, of course, had already propelled Jennifer into international stardom. Both careers were soaring.

In March 1996, Jennifer and Joanna Lumley jetted to Los Angeles for guest appearances at the annual American Comedy Awards, a rare accolade for Brit comedy performers but an indication of the impact *Ab Fab* was having on the wider world.

'I haven't got time in my life to do all the things I should be doing, like running and dieting and decorating my house, buying furniture,' Jennifer said afterwards, although she confessed she'd still somehow managed to find a bit of time for her most absorbing and relaxing domestic passion: gardening.

'I adore gardening. My parents used to love it. And as a teenager, I was always being woken up to the sound of the wheelbarrow outside. And I thought: "I'm never going to get into gardening." But now I love it!'

At the end of 1996, despite all previous protestations to the contrary, *Ab Fab* was back on British TV screens. A BBC1 special, divided into two 45-minute episodes and costing a reported £1 million to produce, went out early in November, entitled *Absolutely Fabulous: The Last Shout*.

The special edition was touted as the definitive end to all adventures for Edina and Patsy – Edina had a close call on the ski slopes and entered heaven, only to meet a singing God (played by Marianne Faithfull in a trouser suit), and Saffy got engaged, much to Edina's horror. Other guests in the special included Edina's favourite designers, Christian Lacroix and Bruce Oldfield.

'It's been a great joy to do and I'll miss the characters,'

said Jennifer. 'But the show would only continue to lose impact. Other shows would replace it. It would become an imitation of life itself. You would start acting up in it rather than acting *in* it. And I won't miss the pain of writing it. I loved dressing up in stupid clothes and being ridiculous and I'm delighted that I've got a fantastic friendship with Joanna Lumley out of it, but it really was time for *Ab Fab*'s funeral.'

Ab Fab fans and, of course, the BBC were now getting used to this kind of comment. No one gave up hope that the series would eventually return. The BBC made no secret of the fact that the door for more *Ab Fab* remained open; after all, it remained one of the broadcaster's best-loved comedies.

Nonetheless, the 'on again, off again' nature of the statements about the series did confuse everyone, including the press.

'Viewers may have been confused by this special edition spread over two nights simply because we had been informed, in no uncertain terms, by star and creator Jennifer Saunders, that the last series was *definitely* the last,' said the *Observer*'s Barbara Ellen.

'Clearly when Saunders says "definitely" she really means "perhaps", which is good news for us, as, though overlong and weaker than Edina's grasp on reality in some places, there were enough vicious one-liners and outbreaks of unapologetic hedonism to ensure that US networks continue to keep their touchy feely bargepoles to themselves.

'Together, Saunders and Lumley have created a comedy double act that is part Hinge and Bracket (in Versace) and part *Withnail and I*. And with good-quality drugs.' (Hinge and Bracket were female impersonators George Logan and Patrick Fyffe, a popular TV and radio double act who were successful in radio and TV in the 1970s and early 1980s.)

The Last Shout went down a storm in the US.

'Saunders has written one of her best *Ab Fab* scripts here. There are unforgettable slapstick scenes of Edina and Patsy skiing at Val d'Isère and some of the choicest insults in *Ab Fab*'s history (Patsy's put-down to Saffron: "She is a virgin in a world where men will even turn to soft fruit for pleasure"),' said American TV and popular culture critic Joyce Millman.

However, not everyone was convinced back in the UK. *Scotland on Sunday* said this 'final' episode of *Ab Fab* was 'an idea well past its sell-by date'.

Afterwards, Jennifer did admit that the programme was 'disjointed, but I just had to get rid of all those jokes I'd always wanted to do. It would have been tragic to look back in 2000 and think: "I wish I'd done that."'

As for negative criticism, her response was: 'I'm my own worst critic. I could tell the critics a thing or two about my shows. Anyway, *Ab Fab* satisfies the fans. People love Edina and Patsy. They do everything people would like to do but would be arrested for it. It's the getting away with it that people like. People look at them and think: "I wish I could say that."'

Despite their huge popularity, however, Jennifer insisted the two women were not intended to be role models for others.

'They aren't successful, they're actually rather sad,' she

told James Rampton in an interview for the *Independent* in 1996. 'They're triers whose lives aren't that great. Edina is always looking for ways to make herself more interesting, she is always searching for "The Life". She believes that attaching herself to something important will make her important in some way. She thinks: "Because I'm a Buddhist, it means I'm important."

'No it doesn't. It means she takes her shoes off. Where she is never good enough – which is a modern disease.'

More *Ab Fab*, of course, meant even more attention for Jennifer when off-camera. Yet again, she openly admitted she didn't like being recognised: 'You get talked at and shouted at. You get fed up being famous because people look at you a lot. It's not debilitating but it's vaguely depressing. It makes me think twice about going to public places. I do the shopping but I wouldn't take the kids to a public swimming pool.'

Maybe part of her dislike for this aspect of her success is a generational thing, a consequence of growing up at a time when youth was less inclined to be attention-seeking and upfront – and often young girls were still expected to be reasonably well behaved and remain on the sidelines.

By the 1990s, of course, there was a totally different generation of young women around, who were mostly unaware of the idea of modesty or self-effacement: the 'me' generation, fully immersed in a diet of consumerism and pop music, young girls who were happy to throw themselves right into the spotlight – and soak up every bit of attention or, if they could grab it, fame.

Confident, bouncy, and unashamedly up for it, 'girl

power' stormed the pop music charts – and the hearts and minds of millions of fans – in 1996, in the shape of five young all-singing, all-dancing bundles of manic, in-yer-face energy: the Spice Girls.

With their cute pop nicknames and their skimpy, glittery gear, Posh, Baby, Sporty, Scary and Ginger burst forth onto the pop scene with unprecedented verve: their first hit single, 'Wannabe', shot them to global attention, the most successful ever debut single of its time. And in the summer of 1996, just before they hit the big time, they forged a relationship with Jennifer and Dawn.

'When they were making their first single, Dawn and I were having lunch near a big recording studio in south-west London and these five odd-looking girls appeared, squealing: "Look, it's French and Saunders,"' recalled Jennifer. 'We've been friends ever since.'

By February 1997, there were very few people on the planet who didn't know who the Spice Girls were – and the five girls cheerfully joined forces with Dawn, Jennifer and Kathy Burke for their side-splitting spoof as Spice wannabes, The Sugar Lumps, to record that year's new Comic Relief single, 'Who Do You Think You Are?', as the girl band reached number one in the US with 'Wannabe'.

With Jennifer as 'Ginger' (Geri Halliwell), Dawn as an unlikely 'Posh' (Victoria Beckham), Lulu as 'Baby' (Emma Bunton) and Kathy Burke as 'Sporty' (Melanie Chisholm), the recording marked the beginning of the professional relationship between Jennifer and the Spice Girls.

At the time, Jennifer's young daughters, then aged 11, 10 and 8, were very much the right age to enjoy the Spice Girls.

'The Spice Girls made them feel better about being female as they were growing up. Girl power made them believe they could be fat or thin, or anything they wanted to be,' recalled Jennifer later.

In June 1997, the Spice Girls started filming *Spice World* in London. Jennifer's brief cameo appearance in the movie (as a younger version of a fashionista, Edina-style, reeling off a designer list – 'Gucci, Pucci, Prada, Fendi' – to a very young 'Posh' Spice, who was obviously taking it all in) meant there was a golden opportunity for her girls to meet their heroines on the set. (It's not too hard to picture the scene chez Edmondson: 'You can only meet the Spice Girls if you tidy your room'.)

However, Jennifer's input into the Spice Girls' lives went beyond the cameo and the fundraising spoof – she even advised her long-term colleague and *Ab Fab* director, the late Bob Spiers, to take the job of directing the movie. And while *Spice World*, a light comic romp with echoes of The Beatles' 1964 film *A Hard Day's Night*, was panned universally by the critics after its release at the end of the year, it proved a huge international success at the box office.

Jennifer also turned up in the celebrity audience for *An Audience with The Spice Girls*, the girls' one-hour ITV special in November 1997.

Accompanied this time by Ella and Freya, it was a tantalisingly brief glimpse of Jennifer as a mum, particularly when 11-year-old Ella was called up by the Spice Girls to ask them her question – 'Are girls better than boys?' (as if...) – and, oh so briefly, Jennifer flashed her eldest daughter that slightly nervous, protective look of mums everywhere just before Ella confidently stood up in front of the audience.

It was the first time a pop group had hosted the popular 'An Audience with' format – and a rare, if revealing, moment that caught the very normal, everyday side of Jennifer's life that she and Ade referred to occasionally – but were mostly careful to protect from any exposure to the wider world.

There were other brief TV appearances in 1997: in May as Jennifer and Dawn lunched with the 1990s comic duo of Mel Giedroyc and Sue Perkins on the Channel 4 daytime series *Light Lunch*, and in November when the *Ab Fab* trio of Jennifer, June Whitfield and Joanna Lumley lunched with Mel and Sue again on the lunchtime programme.

In 1997 there was also a chance to team up again briefly with The Comic Strip gang to film *Four Men in a Car*, a tale of four salesmen en route to a sales conference. Stranded, they wind up in a remote farmhouse, where they encounter Helen, played by Jennifer, an alcoholic diabetic, whose medicine is destroyed by a typically bungling Nigel Planer. The film was shown on Channel 4 on Easter Monday 1998 – and is generally regarded as one of the more successful of *The Comic Strip Presents* series.

At the start of 1998, Jennifer had secured a role in the hugely popular US TV series *Friends,* which ran on Channel 4 from 1994 to 2004. It was suggested by Channel 4 that part of the series could be set in London because one of the characters was engaged to an English girl. As a result, Jennifer teamed up with Tom Conti to play Andrea and Steven Waltham, the very English parents of Emily Waltham (Helen Baxendale) at her London marriage to Ross Geller (David Schwimmer) in two specially devised UK episodes filmed before an audience in London. The British episodes were eventually shown in the UK in May 1998.

'We are the Brits you love to hate: it's the "let's kick the Brits up the butt episode",' said Tom Conti of his role as Jennifer's husband.

Alongside *Ab Fab*'s June Whitfield, making a brief appearance as a snooty housekeeper, Jennifer's portrayal of a bitchy social climber whose contempt for her hubby knows no bounds worked perfectly.

But if 1998 was an important year for Jennifer insofar as her growing fame and celebrity outside the UK were concerned, there was also a significant personal landmark.

In July, she celebrated her fortieth birthday, the age when most people start to reflect on their lives and focus on their achievements – or lack of them – so far.

For some women, reaching the milestone of the fourth decade and saying farewell to their youth is a tough, hard-hitting time. Others sail through it: the old adage 'life begins at 40' rings true for many, so how did turning 40 affect Jennifer?

Outwardly, there was everything to celebrate: good looks (always stunningly attractive, at this point she slimmed down slightly, looking remarkably glowing and confident in her skin), worldly success, a stable marriage, a small but loyal circle of showbiz friends, three beautiful children, two large homes and considerable financial security (Jennifer has never talked publicly about her finances, although Ade told an interviewer he and his wife were 'filthy rich' as far back as 1986).

Yet, at this turning point, her concerns remained pretty much the same as you would expect from any woman. With a dash of Jennifer-type self-deprecation. 'It does set you thinking a bit,' she admitted in an interview with the *Mirror* towards the end of 1998. 'Only because you have an idea about people who are 40. When I started writing *Ab Fab* and Edina turned 40 in the first series I thought it seemed very old. Around the same time, Dawn and I signed a five-year contract with the BBC and I thought: "God, I'll be 40 when it finishes."

'It actually doesn't make much difference except you think that the amount of time you've got left to achieve things is fizzing away.'

There were, she told the *Mirror*, many things she wanted to do. 'But I'm so lazy. I'd like to have written the *Ab Fab* film, done it, directed it, had it out now, then be on to another film and start on the next series and have done that. I think: "What have I done? Messed around for the last five years having a nice life when I should have taken myself more seriously and done more work."

'The trouble is, I find it very hard to pressurise myself.'

Statements like this underline the fact that Jennifer's priorities hadn't been shifted by *Ab Fab*'s success. Family life and husband and a good work-life balance – tick. An important and successful working relationship with Dawn, which, by now, had morphed into separate careers at times but remained solidly loyal. Another tick. As for the admission about not taking herself too seriously, this too merits a tick:

the preoccupation with ego and career has always run rampant through the worlds of television and entertainment.

What she seemed to be saying at this point was: I know who I am, what I value and where I care to be. Yes, I could work harder, run around creating lots of noise and brouhaha, like others, but that's not really who I am.

Nonetheless, the external pressure to up the ante career-wise remained consistent. For one thing, the Americans were still pressing Jennifer to write the *Ab Fab* movie.

'They're desperate for it. I think we could do it if it was directed slickly enough,' she said.

Writing, however, remained a sticking point.

'I hate writing. I love being on TV because it's such good fun making the shows. I keep writing because otherwise you really wouldn't be employed an awful lot,' she told the *Mirror* newspaper. 'It's not like Dawn and I are the greatest actresses or whatever. You write for your own strengths. It's quite nice writing with her and I've enjoyed writing with Ruby Wax. [Ruby has remained a consistent collaborator and script editor over the years.] But I don't like writing for someone else. You think: I'm doing all these bloody good lines for someone else who's probably going to cut them. That's awful.'

Having a deadline was really the only way to get the work done, Jennifer revealed. 'If I'm in the office alone I can easily spend two hours playing games on my computer and that's not a very productive way of getting scripts written, is it?'

But somehow, the scripts did get written. In November 1998, Jennifer made an appearance on BBC1 as herself, in *Absolutely Fabulous: The Collection*, where, as the writer of the show, she introduced the audience to a series of highlights and greatest hits, with each of the three separate programmes focusing in turn on Patsy, Saffy and mother.

And the end of 1998 saw a BBC1 half-hour *French and Saunders* Christmas special, with one of Dawn and Jennifer's most wickedly funny movie spoofs of all time: 'The Making of Titanic the Motion Picture', featuring 'Kate Winslow' as Rose (Jennifer) and 'Leonardo da Vinci' as Jack (Dawn) playing the star-crossed lovers, as well as Dawn and Jennifer playing a number of other lesser roles as crew and extras.

Introduced by a slickly cheesy Joanna Lumley – and with Ade on especially good form as the harassed director 'James Macaroon' – there was even a very brief guest slot from the Spice Girls: classic *French and Saunders*.

May Bank Holiday 1999 saw another BBC1 special from the duo: this included parodies of Boyzone, Catatonia and Alanis Morissette. Most notable were the 'Witless Silence' send-up of the TV show *Silent Witness* with Kathy Burke, and a memorable guest appearance from Helen Mirren in an 'Acting Masterclass' parody, where the star of *Prime Suspect* (and later *The Queen*) played an acting teacher in a canny, sharp satire of the luvvie profession.

In September of that year, Jennifer revealed that, despite many major defections from the BBC at the time, she and Dawn had renewed their contractual obligations to the Beeb – for up to six years. Other big names, including Des Lynam and Noel Edmonds, had quit the BBC and taken the big shilling on offer from commercial television. But the girls decided to stick to the tried and trusted.

'We've had offers to move elsewhere, offers that would quadruple our income, but we have decided that we're well paid for what we do and are not tempted by massive wonga to work for other stations,' said Dawn.

'If you write and perform as we do, you have to be somewhere where you can do what you want. I can't see a single reason to go: we take risks and they let us do it. And the results have been good. Nearly all the great comedies are on the BBC, unless they are American ones,' added Jennifer.

'The BBC is a grown-up place. It still has intellectual programmes and some of its bosses are mavericks, who will take risks. We like the BBC; it's our favourite place. If you are a creative programme maker it still offers the best resources, the most freedom.'

The BBC bosses were, naturally, chuffed. And you can see the wise thinking behind Jennifer and Dawn's decision. They retained a certain amount of freedom to work elsewhere, provided they honoured their contractual obligations to the BBC. And while the big money on offer from commercial television would always sound tempting, it came at a price they had no truck with: ratings pressure, with executives breathing down their necks all the time, interfering and possibly stifling creativity.

They hadn't started out that way and the BBC had always respected that, knowing full well, of course, that by then, whatever the ups and downs of their creative output, their enormous popularity – fuelled by their respective solo successes – meant that the nation would continue to conduct its long love affair with them. Which is exactly what happened.

That summer of 1999, Jennifer and Dawn had been busy filming again. This time it was a new six-part comedy series for the BBC, *Let Them Eat Cake*. Set in the court of Louis XVI of France, in the pre-Revolutionary era, Jennifer played the aristocratic Columbine, Comtesse de Vache, the most reviled woman in France. Dawn was her oversexed maid, Lisette, and Alison Steadman starred as Madame de Plonge, Columbine's greatest rival.

'The liaisons were dangerous, the wigs were lethal' ran a promotional line for the comedy. With lots of elaborate costumes, powdered wigs, heaving bosoms, risqué scenarios and a very large budget, *Cake* should have been an uproarious barrel of laughs. Yet, in the end, it was the reviews that were lethal.

'Dawn French and Jennifer Saunders are one of our top comedy double acts. But you'd never have guessed it from their latest offering, *Let Them Eat Cake*, a spoof on 18th-century French royalty,' said *People* magazine after *Cake* was first shown on BBC1 in September 1999. It was high on ridiculous costumes and low on real humour. Most of the jokes were crude and tasteless. And some seemed as old as the setting.'

'In Peter Learmouth's script, Versailles is populated by thick aristos with ludicrously high coiffures and correspondingly low morals and their sly-boots servants. The humour relies heavily on blunt double entendres (big laughs when Saunders' husband is alluded to as "the old Comte") but there are also numerous references to goitre and "the pox". As in

Blackadder, the past is viewed, not unreasonably, as a Third World country with appalling sanitary arrangements,' said the *Independent*'s Robert Hanks.

The show had been billed as one of the highlights of BBC1's autumn schedule, so its poor critical reception came as a blow. But this was someone else's script – highly unusual for French and Saunders – and, behind the scenes during filming, Dawn had been having an especially difficult time: the tabloids had laid siege to her home over newspaper stories about Lenny and other women.

So while *Cake* was being filmed, Jennifer was doing her level best to help her friend through the trauma of a huge media storm, support Dawn has always appreciated at such a tough time.

'I will never forget the cloak of protection you flung around me when the press were on my tail trying to exacerbate an already sensitive and tricky situation with Len and me,' she wrote in *Dear Fatty*. 'We'd just started a new sitcom, *Let Them Eat Cake*, at the BBC and I was trying to be light-hearted and funny, when I was actually feeling hounded and anxious for Len. 'You were like a gladiator, fiercely guarding me, and calling for coffee breaks whenever you sensed I was a bit wobbly.'

But there was nothing remotely wobbly about Jennifer's workload that year. By the end of 1999, she had turned up in a number of guest or cameo appearances in film and on television.

Along with Stephen Fry, she contributed to the BBC1 children's TV series *The Magician's House*, based on a popular series of children's books written by William

Corlett. The series went out in October 1999, with Jennifer as the voice of the Rat and Fry the voice of Jasper the Owl.

The following month, the London Film Festival screened the premiere of *Fanny and Elvis*, in which Jennifer made a cameo appearance as a bitchy literary agent. A romcom set in the pretty Yorkshire town of Hebden Bridge, the film starred Kerry Fox and Ray Winstone as a pair of unlikely lovers and was scripted by top TV writer Kay Mellor.

'It's quite a small part,' said Jennifer of her literary agent role. 'She's pompous and wants her client to do exactly what she wants. Totally urban, totally London, can't stand Yorkshire – the idea of being in the country is totally abhorrent to her. She's not looking for a masterpiece, she's looking for a bit of sexy trash.'

For all Jennifer's urban Edina-ness, *Fanny and Elvis* was essentially a 'happily ever after' story, and, despite its provenance, the movie didn't have much impact; it was generally regarded as 'too telly' for a big cinema audience.

Jennifer also appeared as herself in December 1999 in an unusual BBC 'Omnibus' documentary entitled *Jennifer Saunders at the Barre*. In it, Jennifer explored the ballet world – and talked about her love of dressing up in character. The general idea of the programme was her quest for inspiration for a sitcom character, ex-ballerina 'Maggie Fontana'.

With the help of real stars of the ballet world, Darcey Bussell and Lynn Seymour, Jennifer learned more about ballerinas – and their feet. She also met veteran choreographer Gillian Lynne, putting the cast of *Cats* through their paces. Jennifer briefly joined the chorus line of the Northern Ballet Theatre and discovered that anyone hoping to get the ballet 'look' should wear cardigans with holes – and ripped Lycra.

Both Jennifer and Dawn wrote and performed a special skit (playing the part of two performers at the Millennium Dome's Body Zone, dressed as eggs in spherical costumes) for BBC1's *The Nearly Complete and Utter History of Everything*, a humorous look at Britain's history, shown on 4 January 2000. But it was their 30-minute end-of-year Christmas special, shown on BBC1 on 28 December 1999, that delighted the fans – and showed the pair very much back on form again, with a much-hyped movie spoof, 'The Phantom Millennium', a *Star Wars: The Phantom Menace* parody, with Dawn playing Toby-Jugs Kenobi (the Ewan McGregor role in the movie) and Jennifer as an impressive Qui-Gon Jinn (the movie's Liam Neeson role, complete with Irish accent). There were also first-rate send-ups of the Spice Girls' Melanie C and Martine McCutcheon.

Yet again, the critics sharpened their pencils with the 'too self-indulgent' criticisms. 'Happily not very Christmassy though not quite special enough either,' was the comment from Kathryn Flett in the *Observer*. 'Their finest moment, however, came with "The Schoolgirls", who are always delicately, touchingly bathetic.'

The audiences, however, were not deterred at all; they lapped it up.

In May 2000, the BBC announced that the *Ab Fab* team would be back on Britain's TV screens – only this time they'd be in a brand-new comedy series called *Mirrorball*, which would be directed by Ade.

The team had already filmed a pilot episode and now there were plans for it to run to six episodes in 2001. After immersing herself in the ballet world the previous year, Jennifer had been inspired to write a new series where the focus would be switched from sending up the fashion and media worlds to spoofing the vagaries of the acting profession.

Jennifer confessed that she was somewhat nervous about the new venture, mainly because of the obvious comparisons with *Ab Fab*. 'It's hard to have something that was such a success because in other people's minds, nothing will be acceptable,' she said. 'And you can't remember what it was that was ever funny. You watch it going why, why are they laughing?'

There was more news that summer. In August, it was widely reported that Jennifer and Ade's production company, Mr and Mrs Monsoon, had placed the couple amongst the UK's wealthiest broadcasters, mostly thanks to the international success of *Ab Fab*, although it was also claimed that Jennifer had refused to sell off advertising and merchandising rights to the show for fear the characters would lose credibility. (It was suggested at the time that Jennifer and Ade were worth in the region of £10 million, although neither ever confirmed this.)

In September 2000, Jennifer and Dawn guested in a 70-minute BBC1 documentary, *Night of a Thousand Shows*, a celebration of the fortieth anniversary of BBC Television Centre, presented by Michael Parkinson. And by then, the girls' big news was already out: for the first time in decades, they would be once again hitting the road on a very big tour of the UK.

To promote the tour, *French and Saunders: Live in 2000*, the pair made a guest appearance on Parkinson's chat show. It was a revealing interview in that Jennifer, clearly uneasy and nervous about her appearance as herself, openly admitted to Parky that she didn't like interviews – 'I'm really not very good at them' – and despite looking extremely svelte and chic in her customary all-black outfit, she informed a curious host that she worried about what she looked like – 'I worry about most things,' she added ruefully.

Dawn, exuberant as usual and openly in total thrall to fellow guest, singer Tom Jones – later in the show she presented him with some very large pairs of knickers – was as vibrant, confident and entertaining as ever. But Jennifer's unease was painfully obvious.

Her body language, arms tightly crossed as if protecting herself, told some of the story: here was a complex person, an enormously successful, acclaimed comic entertainer uneasy with her fame. This obvious reticence might have been baffling for her armies of fans. And, of course, her on-camera discomfort duly translated into fodder for newspaper critics. But none of this would make any difference at all to her profile. By now, it was established: Jennifer Saunders had become a very big star indeed.

French and Saunders: Live in 2000 opened at the beginning of October in Manchester. It took in 20 cities and over 50 dates at big venues right across the country.

The grand finale, the girls' first appearance on a London stage together since *Me and Mamie O'Rourke*, was a four-week-long run at London's Hammersmith Apollo in November.

Compared with their 1989 tour, the *Live in 2000* road show was an enormous operation: 40-foot lorries transporting massively extravagant sets, state-of-the-art projectors and lighting rigs. Teams of roadies. Posh hotel suites. More like a superstar rock performer's extravaganza – and, of course, a sell-out, all dates.

Promoter Phil McIntyre admitted that he had constantly tried to persuade them to consider a new tour, but he had had to be very, very patient. 'They always sort of said yes, but never put a time frame on it,' said McIntyre.

'He's been asking us to do it for eight years, but we have families now so it was difficult to find a long enough stretch of free time,' explained Jennifer. 'We started planning it a year ago. We love playing live but it takes a lot of time and planning.'

'It was a very good, drunken tour, that one,' said McIntyre, recalling the 1989 tour. 'But things are more sober this time. The girls still like to go out nightclubbing but they just can't do it as often.'

This time, the show combined the girls' sketches with use of the latest technical equipment. The set, according to Jennifer, was 'very Tate Modern' because the 'audiences would get very bored these days with just us and a couple of stools as props.'

Very much a visual spectacular, the show included pre-recorded sketches that were relayed to the audience on a large video screen at the back of the stage, with which the pair could interact throughout.

There were take-offs of Ann Widdecombe and Liz Taylor by Dawn and a fantastic spoof on Liz Hurley from Jennifer. Jennifer's pole-dancing gig with a very large strap-on brassiére brought the house down, as did the incisive TV send-ups of *Casualty* (where the girls played extras) and *Who Wants To Be A Millionaire?* And the material moved away from their older routines – where they would often pretend to be children – and focused more on the concerns of their own generation, i.e. 40-somethings with kids.

'The duo's new stage act is superb, with hilarious skits about subjects ranging from *Big Brother* to breakfast telly ("PM TV"),' raved Glasgow's *Sunday Mail*.

And aside from one or two sniffy broadsheet reviews – claiming the extensive use of technology made the duo seem 'less real' – audiences and reviewers were both in accord this time: the big tour was an unqualified success. But how successful was it for Jennifer?

'As soon as we got back on stage, we thought: "This is where we want to be,"' said Jennifer.

Yet the rigours of several months spent touring, separated from Ade and her girls, now 14, 13 and 10, affected her much more than she had imagined.

'My kids are very supportive of my career, they seem to like what I do. But I find it difficult to leave them at home and go on the road. I thought that as they got older, they'd need me less, but they need me more now. And I miss them,' she said.

Spending so much time working with Dawn, however, helped compensate for this in one way.

'I think there's probably a healthy competition on stage, so that the show has an edge,' said Jennifer. 'But we are not in any way jealous of each other on stage or off.'

Looking back over the 20 years of their partnership, she admitted that, while their public act – with Jennifer usually playing the quieter, smaller one and Dawn the larger, more talkative and effusive one – remained pretty much as it always had been, in private their personalities had now changed quite a lot.

'She's changed enormously since we first started working together. She had the biggest diary in her handbag that I've ever seen and I always had to rely on her to know what we were doing,' admitted Jennifer in an interview with the *Daily Mail*. 'Dawn used to take care of everything but that's changed in that she's become much more easy-going and now I'm the one who has to bully her into working.

'She's generally much more relaxed now, which I think comes from security – she used to buzz around a lot. 'She's the kind of person people love to see, touch, like to talk to and feel part of, whereas I can't understand why someone who doesn't know me would want to come over and talk to me.'

Jennifer also paid homage to Dawn's resilience: 'When she had a few problems last year she just kept on working. She has an incredible strength that carries her through difficult times.'

Motherhood, of course, had also made a huge difference.

'I always knew she would be a natural mother. Kids love her. She is godmother to my eldest daughter and she never forgets her birthday. I actually have to say to my children: "When were you born?" But Dawn never forgets a birthday or an anniversary.'

Just as the tour wound up, the pilot episode of *Mirrorball* went out on BBC1 on 22 December.

Jennifer had created some interesting-sounding characters for the planned series, which she had dubbed 'a romp through the world of failure'. She played Vivienne Keill, an unsuccessful actress who mostly worked as a waitress. Joanna Lumley was again her best friend, cabaret performer Jackie Riviera, and Julia Sawalha was Vivienne's more successful sister. June Whitfield was also in the cast as Vivienne's mother.

But *Mirrorball* bombed. It never went beyond the pilot. Despite the assembled talent, there just weren't many laughs. (There had been plans to screen the six-part series on Comedy Central in the US, where *Ab Fab* had been so successful, but since the series was never concluded, only the pilot episode was screened in the States, on cable channel BBC America.)

Some reviews were scathing. The *Mirror* described it as: 'a decidedly shaky pilot for a series which just doesn't look as if it will ever fly. Most of the characters were *Ab Fab* clones: Saunders as a neurotic dancer past her best, Joanna Lumley as a drug-taking, fag-puffing mad cow of a singer. It flopped because there simply were not enough good jokes to go round.'

Disappointed fans, however, were not going to be downhearted for very long. Because even before the *Mirrorball* pilot had been shown, *Ab Fab*'s millions of fans heard the words they had desperately hoped to hear for five years: *Ab Fab* was on its way back.

Early in December, Jennifer announced in the *Telegraph* that a new series would be screened in 2001, with all the original cast.

'We had such a great time making *Mirrorball* that we all wanted to work together again. 'But when I sat down to write the new characters I felt Patsy and Edina and all the other *Ab Fab* characters vying for my attention. So in the end I gave in – and I'm looking forward to moving the characters into the new millennium, and adding a few new ones.'

But there was another reason for recreating *Ab Fab* again: its success in America.

'America was so cheerful about it because in America they just think things go on and on, and why shouldn't you? And you get infected by that and you think: "Yeah, why shouldn't I do another one?" Because if you can think of enough good jokes – and generally I think there are more jokes than in the average sitcom – then why don't we do it? And we generally have a really great time making it. We have such a bloody laugh. And if I could just do that and it never went out, I would be so happy for the rest of my life.'

It's a highly improbable, even laughable scenario: Jennifer Saunders spending her time making TV shows that no one would ever see. Yet it's obvious where she was coming from – having fun with family and friends has always been the priority. No amount of success would change that. And there would be plenty of fun and good times in the pipeline. Because at this point, Jennifer and Ade were planning to

capitalise on their success and enjoy their lives even more –
as far away from the glare of media intrusion as they could
possibly manage.

CHAPTER 6

GOING
GREEN

At the beginning of 2001, Jennifer and Dawn were offered the OBE (Order of the British Empire) for Services to Comedy Drama. They quietly turned it down but the news was somehow leaked to the press anyway.

'If I felt I'd deserved damehood, I'd accept it,' said Jennifer later. 'We were being paid very well to have fun. We didn't deserve a pat on the back. It would have felt fake to stand alongside people who devote their lives to much more worthy causes.'

In March 2001, she and Dawn appeared in a poignant BBC1 music tribute, *The Life and Lyrics of Kirsty MacColl*. Accompanied by Bono, Billy Bragg, Jools Holland, Cerys Matthews and Shane MacGowan, the performers paid homage to the immensely popular singer-songwriter who had been tragically killed in a controversial boating incident in Mexico in December 2000.

Filming of the long-awaited new *Ab Fab* series began in May. This time, Edina was lurching into a different career, with her own production company called Radical TV.

Using *Ab Fab*'s role as a mirror to the social zeitgeist, the new series, five years on, would obviously have to underline Edina's and Patsy's desperate, unending quest to be involved with the latest trend or fad.

'The idea of celebrity is probably the biggest change in the new series,' said Jennifer. 'Fashion is now just another service industry – you can get Gucci in the supermarket. But what has taken over is this celebrity feeding frenzy.

'Eddy's got a production company because it seems everyone has one of those. We've turned into a world of minor celebs, famous for reading off the autocue.'

Given her infrequent appearances at big celebrity gatherings, how did Jennifer research this world?

'By six months of really intense magazine reading,' she told the *Independent* newspaper in 2001. 'I did visit *Heat* magazine. Actually, I was incredibly disappointed. I thought they might be a bit bitchier but they seemed quite nice. I was hoping for edge, but it was edgeless. And before I wrote it, I had to call in the earlier scripts to make sure I didn't repeat anything.'

Some of the scenes were filmed on location in Paris, including a shopping-and-drinking trip on the Champs-Élysées and a flashback episode going back to the 1960s. As far as her own recreation of Edina was concerned, Jennifer remained quite critical of her acting skills.

'I really cringe about some bits, almost always when I'm overacting. I watch all the other cast members and I'm really impressed. Then I watch me and make a mental note to myself: must try harder. Often I'll wish I didn't go for the immediate laugh. But it's so tempting to do.'

For the new series, she had created a new character called Katy Grin, a TV presenter played by Jane Horrocks (with an eerie resemblance to Anthea Turner).

'Being a presenter has become a real career option. I find presenter-worship really extraordinary. But the turnover is pretty quick. You know they're doing every single job they can until the juice runs out and then there's complete disbelief when they find out that the public doesn't love them,' said Jennifer.

Ruby Wax's input into script editing such aspects of *Ab Fab* proved, as always, invaluable.

'Ruby's very good on the whole idea of fame and how people try to squeeze the last minutes out of it when they get to a certain age.'

Nor would Patsy and Edina, despite all their efforts, be able to revive their never-very-youthful glow. 'It's 10 years since we started and people do get on, get slightly more morose, too old to be thrashing around on the town,' Jennifer said in the *Independent* interview of 2001. 'Also, we used to get a laugh on words like "colonic". But nowadays everything is available at your local health spa. Everyone can get acupuncture. So what we're concentrating on is more the psychological side: my mother was hopeless with me, Edina's hopeless with Saffy, that sort of thing.

'The gay community, particularly in America, became obsessed with the sweetie, Bolly, fags stuff, but I've tried to get rid of it a bit in this series,' she added.

As for Eddy's 'look', Jennifer admitted that she was now exercising a certain amount of caution over the loud, attention-grabbing outfits she wore for the early *Ab Fab* episodes.

'Like Eddy, I've got quite a young taste in clothes. My daughter, Beattie, is 14 now and I caught myself admiring her trainers,' she revealed to the *People*. 'Luckily, she thinks the way I dress is quite cool. But there are certain things I have to say no to. At my age [nearly 43] there's no way I'm going to wear a top that shows off my midriff. Or the tops of my arms.

'Someone did once suggest Eddy wear a crop top – but I put my foot down!'

Celebrity guests this time included Dale Winton, Richard and Judy, Twiggy, and Lady Victoria Hervey. 'With celebrity cameos we draw up a hit list of people to approach, then in the end about three people agree. It's hard to write a scene that will actually work. You want to use that person but you don't want to throw the programme out of balance. Twiggy is one of my favourite guests – so much fun, we extended her role.'

At one point, Eddy and Patsy emerge as very old women, following several hours in makeup and with help from specially constructed prosthetic masks.

'It's very strange to see yourself aged like that – because we know that is exactly what we'll look like,' said Jennifer ruefully.

But a fear even worse than that of ageing, one familiar to comedy writers and performers since time immemorial, remained ever present at the back of Jennifer's mind throughout the creation of the newest *Ab Fab*.

'Everyone will be out to judge it,' she admitted. 'I do feel a certain amount of fear, fear that the moment it's committed to paper it might no longer be funny.'

She was wrong. Age and time had not diminished the comic potential of the antics of the outrageous Ab Fabbers; they remained as riotously entertaining as ever. Eight million BBC viewers tuned in to the series in September 2001. The reviews this time were mixed. Some critics liked it; others complained it wasn't up-to-date enough.

'When it [Ab Fab] arrived in the middle of the last recession, the idea of lampooning the fashion and PR businesses was not just a potentially smart idea, it was also dead easy to do,' commented the Observer's Kathryn Flett. 'But in the boom years since then we've all arguably caught up with Patsy and Edina to become an equally vapid, trivial nation of designer label consumers, vicarious star fuckers and fashion victims. So, there's even less to laugh at now that it's failing to keep ahead of the game.'

'The show still surfs the zeitgeist with jokes about micro-scooters, life coaches, yoga, internet porn and allusions to Botox injections but it all seems rather obvious and out of date,' carped the Guardian.

As for the guest appearances, the Guardian added: 'Ab Fab seems to be more in awe of celebrity culture than sceptical about it.'

Curiously enough, the view of the new series from the birthplace of celebrity culture was much more enthusiastic than that in the UK. 'Watching the girls desperately lose their grasp on youthful trendiness is sort of like watching the world's funniest train wreck,' said the Los Angeles

Daily News. 'Fans will be pleased that Patsy and Edina show no ill effects from their five-year lay-off; they're as biliously self-absorbed as ever.'

By the time the nation was welcoming Edina and Patsy back, however, Jennifer and Ade were on the verge of reaching a big decision they had been toying with for ages: a full-time move to their much-loved home in Devon. So they put their home in south-west London on the rental market and went in search of greater privacy and seclusion, right off the beaten track on the north-eastern edge of Dartmoor, one of the UK's last remaining wilderness areas.

Here, at last, was the chance to live out their rural dream in the open green spaces of the English countryside, the life they had hankered after for so long.

'We were living in London for about 20 years, but everything we wanted to do was in Devon – being in an open, lovely house with terrific views, with a few sheep, cows and horses in the grounds,' explained Jennifer some time after the move in an interview with the *Mail on Sunday.*

'We were doing it all in the holidays but eventually we just thought: "This is mad, let's do what we want to do every day and only come up to London occasionally."'

'We're remote but not cut off,' she explained in the interview. 'There's a local bus service that goes to Chagford, only 10 minutes away, and the girls can get to Exeter and back quite quickly. We're only half an hour from a train station so I can get to London in under two hours.'

Set in five acres in the area near Chagford and completely secluded, the 400-year-old sprawling granite longhouse, complete with swimming pool and outbuildings, could now be the family's full-time base.

There was plenty of space to create their own 'office' area for the couple's respective writing projects. The girls would be enrolled at a private school in the area and, together with their mum, they could enjoy riding horses out on the wide open spaces of Dartmoor. And their 'neighbours' would include Ade's comedy partner Rik Mayall, in his holiday home 30 miles away on the Devon coast at Kingsbridge.

The Edmondsons were not the only successful showbiz people to be attracted to this beautiful area, which offers both privacy and an inspirational landscape for artistic or creative people: Devon is the only county in England that boasts two historic national parks, Dartmoor and Exmoor. Artist Damien Hirst, Blur singer Damon Albarn and TV's Noel Edmonds are just a few of the well-known names drawn to the area, where locals tend to absorb any well-heeled incomers into their small, rural communities, yet respect their need to live a completely normal life without being constantly pestered by celebrity-hunters and paparazzi.

Horse riding, sailing and traditional English country life were about to supplant more urban pursuits, partly because the couple wanted to give their daughters a rural, less frenetic environment to replace some of the more indoor, urban distractions the now-teenage girls were absorbing in London.

'The middle one, who is 14, just loves the cartoons on the Cartoon Channel – which is my biggest battle at the moment,' said Jennifer in an outburst of criticism of twenty-first-century kids' TV programming. 'It annoys me because I hate the noise. They don't seem to have – it's very old-fashioned – a story. It's like they've forgotten there could be rules. Mass-manufactured animation, so lazy. And I can't stand Pokémon – it's just awful.'

With the green, rural spaces and a much more relaxed way of life in view, the Edmondsons would be enjoying the same kind of country environment Jennifer and Ade had both known as children.

Jennifer's childhood passion for riding horses was undiminished: out on Dartmoor, it's quite simple to commune with nature, go horse riding for hours on end, right out onto open moorland, without anyone around at all – apart from the odd encounter with a few sheep or a Dartmoor pony.

'Our house is very picturesque but not in a pretty way; it's quite wild and high up, but it has a great atmosphere and I love it,' she told the *Mail on Sunday* in 2005.

In a previous interview with the *Daily Mail* in April 2002, she had also revealed her shopping list for their new rural environment. Horse riding, of course, was the main priority. 'I've bought a couple of horses and I'll go to a market and see some lovely ducks and think: "Oooh, I could buy those ducks,"' enthused Jennifer, whose other lifelong passion – cars – could also now be indulged in the traffic-free country lanes, far from the frustration of endless parking meters and fume-clogged, narrow London streets.

'And I'm still looking at the latest Land Rover kind of situation... four-wheel drives, horseboxes, all the things you need in the country,' she told the *Guardian* newspaper in 2001.

In the interview, she also revealed that the girls had been doing sailing courses, much to their father's delight. 'He's got a little boat in Dartmouth. I want an RIB, a hard-bottomed inflatable with a steering wheel – they're kind of fast. It's like having a little runaround on the water. Really good fun.'

Jennifer has frequently extolled her love of the countryside over the years. In a BBC Radio 2 show, she said: 'There's something really nice about the smell of horse and tack. And new-cut grass. I like the countrified thing.'

But while the joys of the wide open spaces and their move preoccupied the Edmondsons during the early 2000s, back in the very contrasting, urban world of Eddy and Patsy, Jennifer found herself defending the some-what scathing critical response to their new *Ab Fab* series after its five-year absence. Yet her perspective remained reasonably sanguine.

'It bothers me for the people who are in it, but I think I accept it because I was sort of expecting it and I'm probably my worst critic. But you have to resign yourself to it, say: "Ah, damn, could do better, must try harder." It also lacks structure. That was my failing. But this series has got some really good things in it.'

Edina, she admitted, was encountering the slippery slope of the ageing process, something she was all too aware of herself.

'There's a real age fear that's kicked in, a real feeling that your life is passing very, very quickly now and you haven't done anything and I think a real panic sets in,' she told the *Guardian*. 'I think I do feel it, probably for the first time this year. I've felt older. I've felt I'm slowly becoming more decrepit. It's when physical things happen. When you try and run 100 yards and find out you're not fit any more. Bad side lighting hits you.

'You start noticing little things. You see a photograph of yourself and think: "Who's that?" That's quite a shock. I think you just move into the country and wear an old fleece. I'm not great at clothes. My friend Betty Jackson looks at me occasionally and says: "You've just got to come into the shop." So I went up [to London] and she gave me a bit of a makeover. I'm not very good at that kind of fiddly stuff.'

Being funny in front of millions often means worrying that it will all stop one day. 'Especially as you get older. You have the idea that humour has changed and what people expect from humour has changed. You don't have an eternal life on television – you have to accept that and do something else.'

Yet by now, it wasn't just the Americans who hankered after their own version of *Ab Fab*. The French had also fallen heavily for Edina and Patsy, with the series a big hit on French cable television. Eventually, the rights to a French movie adaptation of *Ab Fab*, entitled *Absolument Fabuleux* and set in France, were sold and the French version premiered in Paris in August 2001.

Starring comic actress Josianne Balasko as Eddie Mousson (Eddy), Nathalie Baye as Patricia (Patsy) and Marie Gillain as Safrane (Saffy), and written and directed by Gabriel Aghion, Jennifer made a brief cameo appearance

Above left and right: On the set of *Absolutely Fabulous*. Jennifer as Edina, Joanna Lumley as Patsy and Julia Sawalha as Edina's long suffering daughter, Saffy. *©Rex Features*

Below: Jennifer, the creator of *Ab Fab*, with Joanna Lumley celebrating at the British Comedy Awards party. *©Rex Features*

Above: Lifetime friends: Lenny Henry, Dawn, Jennifer and Adrian at the press night of *French and Saunders* on Drury Lane, October 2008.

©*Getty Images*

Below: Enjoying some downtime with Lulu at Jules Holland and Christabel McEwan's wedding.

©*Getty Images*

Supporting fellow actors and comedians.

Above: Jennifer and Joanna with actor Robert Lindsay at the *Lion in Winter* press night.

Below: At the press night for Matthew Bourne's ballet, *Cinderella,* at Sadler's Wells with Jasper Conran (left) and Bruno Tonioli (right).

Jennifer has always had a great relationship with members of the Spice Girls.

Above left: Jennifer as Eddy with 'Baby Spice' (Emma Bunton) in 2011. ©*Getty Images*

Above right: Jennifer teamed up with the Spice Girls in 1997 for Comic Relief. From left: Kathy Burke as 'Sporty Spice' (Mel C), Dawn as 'Posh Spice' (Victoria) and Jennifer as 'Ginger Spice' (Geri). ©*Rex Features*

Below: Celebrating joining forces with the Spice Girls to work on the musical *Viva Forever!* ©*Getty Images*

At the British Comedy Awards in 2004. Jennifer posing with her award for Outstanding
Contribution to Comedy.

©Getty Images

With her most recent award: a BAFTA.
Celebrating with Dawn, Richard Curtis
and Helen Mirren. ©*Getty Images*

Above left: A cause close to her heart: raising money and awareness for breast cancer care and research. Jennifer and Harriet Thorpe, part of Jen's Big Tits Team, taking part in the charity event MoonWalk, London 2012. ©*Rex Features*

Above right: Never one to shy away from displaying her bra... for a good cause! ©*Rex Features*

Below: With a host of other celebrities taking part in the MoonWalk in 2007. ©*Getty Images*

in the French *Ab Fab*, as a fashionista chatting with über-glamorous French movie star Catherine Deneuve at a Jean Paul Gaultier fashion show.

The movie did not do especially well at the French box office. French critics commented that the very British humour in the series didn't quite translate onto the big screen. And this wasn't really surprising. *Ab Fab*, the series, might have crossed several cultural divides when it came to making audiences laugh, but there is a certain uniquely British quality to boozy, drug-taking women acting badly that ran counter to the more traditional, conventional, often ultra-feminine attitudes of French women. Eddy and Patsy are obsessed with girly things – weight, clothes, fashion – but they're not exactly girly in their behaviour.

In March 2002, Jennifer and Dawn were back together on BBC1 in an Easter special, *The Egg*. The 40-minute special – their first since the *Star Wars* spoof in 1999 – drew an audience of 6 million and was essentially a parody of Peter Jackson's huge smash hit movie, *The Lord of the Rings*.

Skewering the complicated mythology and peculiar names of the story, the duo sprang into normal send-up mode halfway through to take potshots at well-known faces including Bono, Harry Potter and, their old favourite, Madonna. The Madonna-as-guest story, of course, had turned into a recurring theme over many years.

'Dawn and I have asked Madonna to do our show ever since we first got a gig on the telly. She always says no, but every year we ask again. Dawn and I ring up her agent just to hear her say: "Sorry, she's touring", "Sorry, she's out of the country" or whatever. So we just put her name down anyway. It's become a little tradition,' said Jennifer.

April saw another international accolade for Jennifer and Dawn: they were the first women ever to be awarded an Honorary Golden Rose Award at the Montreux Festival in Switzerland. At the same time, Jennifer announced that two more *Ab Fab* specials were in the pipeline, one of which would take Edina and Patsy back to their old stomping ground – the Big Apple.

'People are always asking us so I thought we'll do it again,' explained Jennifer.

In June, Whoopi Goldberg presented Jennifer and Joanna Lumley with a special human rights award at a gay pride ceremony in the Big Apple's City Hall – and named the pair honorary New Yorkers. And that same month, Jennifer and Dawn's voices were heard in key roles in *Pongwiffy*, a children's cartoon series shown on ITV from June to September 2002. Based on the successful *Pongwiffy* books by Kaye Umansky, Dawn was the voice of Pongwiffy and Jennifer her best friend, Sharkadder.

Now permanently based in Devon, Jennifer found that having an intermittent relationship with big city life was much more to her liking, a real 'best of both worlds' situation.

'I enjoy London a lot more. I'll come up for one or two days a week and I find that London is so much nicer when you're experiencing it in controlled doses. And my kids certainly don't miss the city,' she told the *Mail on Sunday* in 2005.

Jennifer admitted in the interview that she and Ade wouldn't have moved at all if the girls hadn't agreed to the move: 'They have a lot more freedom in the country. Some of their friends live on farms with barns, so they spend a lot of their time just hanging around in the open – it's much nicer. I don't worry about them at all in Devon.'

Country life lived up to all their original expectations.

'I spend hours at the bottom of the garden making bonfires. I can be there for such a long time Ade has to send out search parties,' she told the *Mail on Sunday*. 'I like a long, slow burn, lots of wet leaves on top, no sudden bursts of flame. Actually, it's when I'm tending bonfires or sweeping – I'm big on sweeping too – that I do most of my thinking. Ade knows a new show may be coming up if there's suddenly a spate of bonfires.'

Christmas saw the first *Ab Fab* special, *Absolutely Fabulous: New York*, shown on BBC1 on 27 December 2002. This time, Eddy and Patsy descended on New York after Patsy left her glossy magazine job to become a buyer for a fashion store and Eddy discovered that her long-lost son, Serge, was living in the city.

Jane Horrocks did an uproarious turn as Lola, a Dolly Parton clone with enormous breasts. And, by sheer accident, Eddy and Patsy were joined in matrimony at a same-sex wedding centre by a counsellor played by Whoopi Goldberg (Jennifer somehow managed to persuade Whoopi to make a tiny cameo appearance in the special, a whistle-stop, brief break from movie-making). With further cameo appearances from Debbie Harry and Graham Norton and the regular cast, including Harriet Thorpe and Helen Lederer, the 2002 *Ab Fab* special pulled in 9 million viewers: one of the BBC's top-rating comedies of the year.

Within weeks, it was announced that a fifth series of *Ab Fab* would be shown later in 2003.

Yet the Edmondsons would now sometimes find that they had to tear themselves away from the tranquillity of their rural retreat for longer periods. Writing a brand-new series requires immense concentration, so it was decided that Jennifer would spend several weeks in London, penning the new *Ab Fab* series, while Ade continued to live the life of a gentleman farmer, complete with smallholding, tractor and a developing passion for hedge-building – a welcome contrast to the intense and competitive jungle of TV and show business.

'I'd rather be lambing and fighting bracken than worrying about ratings and dealing with irritating TV executives,' said Ade, who was continuing to write and make TV appearances in addition to comedy acting roles on stage locally in Exeter.

As for Jennifer's international stardom, taking a back seat to her fame was never in any way going to be a problem in their relationship.

'Sometimes it's nice just to be Mr Jennifer Saunders,' he admitted to the *Mirror* in 2003. 'I like being able to take a backseat.

'People expect me to be jealous of Jennifer but what would you rather have, a superstar for a wife or one who just does the ironing?' he told the *Mirror*. 'When we are booked into a hotel in the States, we are always down as Mr and Mrs Saunders but it doesn't bother me.'

In an interview with the *Daily Mail* in 2003, Ade insisted that their public and private faces were entirely different.

'Everyone thinks Jennifer is this whirlwind of dynamic creative talent, but she spends most of her time dead-heading roses. Most of our life is about gardening and shovelling horse muck.'

At home, Ade revealed the family's culinary preferences were a combination of English and Mediterranean food with lots of roast meats and roast vegetables – 'Jennifer can cook anything. And she's very good with meat.'

'The superwoman image is nothing we know about,' he told the *Mail*. 'She becomes very powerful when she is making her show because she is the central spark and it doesn't happen without her. But we leave all that aside at home.'

In March 2003, Ade and Jennifer joined forces again for a Comic Relief spoof, a delightfully funny send-up of the *Harry Potter* movie, 'Harry Potter and the Secret Chamberpot of Azerbaijan'. Written and directed by Ade, Dawn played Harry Potter, Jennifer was Ron Weasley, and they were joined by author J.K. Rowling, Ronnie Corbett, Basil Brush, Jeremy Irons, Miranda Richardson, Nigel Planer and Alison Steadman in one of the highlights of that year's Red Nose night, the telethon raising a record £35 million.

With a new series of *Ab Fab* underway and two Christmas specials for both *Ab Fab* and *French and Saunders*, 2003 was a full-on year, work-wise, for Jennifer. Yet when she was approached by Hollywood that summer to see if she was interested in voicing the Fairy Godmother in a new *Shrek* movie, *Shrek 2*, the second fairy-tale animated film about the lovable green troll, she instantly accepted – believing, with typical modesty, that nothing would come of it. (The original *Shrek*, the US computer-animated fantasy comedy movie based on a picture book, had won international acclaim, huge box-office success and an Oscar following its release in 2001.)

'I never thought I'd get to do it – I just thought an awful lot of other people must have turned it down. I never normally get asked to do voice-overs, unlike Dawn who has a very expressive, warm voice.

'I loved the first *Shrek* – I thought it was absolute genius. The girls loved it too. It's like the whole *Toy Story* idea where it's animation but it's also a really clever story and it appeals to all age groups.'

In her solo guest appearance on BBC1's *Parkinson* in October 2003, Jennifer seemed slightly more relaxed than during her previous appearance on Parky's show. And she certainly looked every inch the successful international writer/actor in sleekly expensive black leather and shiny boots. Recalling her youthful student era with Dawn, she harked back to the carefree times when they fell into performing, almost by accident.

'The joy of the relationship is you never quite grow up,' she told Michael Parkinson. This time, it was Parky's turn to look quite smitten.

The fifth series of *Ab Fab* started on BBC1 on 17 October 2003, written by Jennifer, script edited by Ruby Wax and with additional material from Sue Perkins. Guests included Emma Bunton, Kristin Scott Thomas, Jeanette Krankie, Mariella Frostrup, Minnie Driver, Elton John and John Paul Gaultier. When a pregnant Saffy returns from Africa to announce that she's going to have a mixed-race baby, Eddy is delighted at the impending arrival of such a fashionable appendage – 'the Chanel of babies'.

Now a celebrity PR with just a handful of clients, including Emma Bunton and Queen Noor of Jordan, she gets busy with installing a new panic room – stocked with spliffs and Bolly, of course.

'I've tried to keep it much more domestic this time,' said Jennifer. 'When you go out and about on location too much it can dilute everything. It's at its best when Edina and Patsy are in the house, totally overreacting.'

As usual, Eddy has yet to tone down her act when it comes to wearing designer gear. This time she sported Jean Paul Gaultier's denim matador jacket and trousers: 'Where the waist is above your tit level and the shoulders above your head,' said Jennifer.

The first two episodes of series five of *Ab Fab* drew audiences of well over 7 million, yet by the time the series ended in December, audiences had dropped off to just under 6 million for the final episode.

As was now becoming almost a rite of passage, criticism of the series was strident: 'More laughs to be had at a Tory Party Conference,' said the *Liverpool Echo*. 'With no clever storylines and only the occasional cutting and witty one-liner, *Ab Fab* is as shallow and vacuous as Edina and Patsy's "characters".'

If Jennifer was getting fed up or in any way discouraged by the repeated accusations that the show was well past its sell-by date, she wasn't especially vocal about it.

And by the end of the year, when two new shows went out on BBC1 over the Christmas period – the *Ab Fab* Christmas special 'Cold Turkey' (a 35-minute episode on 24 December) with guests Kate O'Mara, Eleanor Bron, Miranda Richardson and an early appearance from BBC comedy star Miranda Hart (whose comic talent had been quickly spotted by Jennifer), followed on 26 December by the 40-minute special *French and Saunders Actually*, with spoofs on The White Stripes, Madonna, Britney Spears and Catherine Zeta-Jones – Jennifer was already looking ahead to an exceptionally demanding and exciting 2004.

Because, despite her initial belief that the *Shrek 2* movie part would be offered to someone else, she had landed the Fairy Godmother role. And she was thrilled to be voicing the character in a big Hollywood movie, balancing out the recent bruising reception given to the BBC Christmas specials.

'You're just an ingredient. And no one's going to say: "That movie didn't work because Jennifer Saunders' voice wasn't good." It's so completely liberating! It's lovely. I've no responsibility. This job's one of my favourite jobs in the world. No one's looking at you,' she said.

With an array of big-name voices in various roles, including Mike Myers (as Shrek), Eddie Murphy (Donkey), Antonio Banderas (Puss in Boots), Cameron Diaz (Princess Fiona), John Cleese (King Harold), Julie Andrews (Queen Lillian) and Rupert Everett (Prince Charming), the *Shrek 2* actors did not meet up or work together as a team in any way. Instead, their parts were recorded in tiny booths across different parts of the world.

Jennifer voiced the Fairy Godmother (a monstrous bully with a very Edina-like personality) in London, seated in a small booth, with a camera focused on her face to capture every expression on film. This tape was then sent on to the animators.

'I spent all these weeks inside a box with a very nice man from DreamWorks guiding me through exactly what I had to do,' Jennifer told the *Mail on Sunday* in 2004. 'It's very surreal. You feel that you've just done some stuff and they then go away and pull it all apart and make this fantastic thing. It's like you haven't really been in it. I think it was the most difficult, amazing and most enjoyable thing I've ever done.'

As for the character, with all her glaring imperfections, Jennifer loved her. 'She's just a pushy mum – she just wants that useless son of hers to do better, to be more like her. I was so disappointed at the end that she was going to die, I made them record me saying the line "I'll be back" – but she wasn't.'

Already familiar with voicing characters in animated productions, Jennifer still felt somewhat apprehensive about the quality of her voice.

'I have all these theories about my voice: it's very flat and rather boring,' she confessed to the *Mail on Sunday*. 'So I had this vague idea to "do" the Fairy Godmother as Edina, as obviously my own voice wouldn't do. But I was told very nicely and very repeatedly just to speak as myself.

'My greatest fear, however, was singing. I can sing reasonably well but I always sing as somebody else. Again, they wanted my voice. Me singing as me and I had a big panic about it. I knew my voice would not just be heard but listened to in massive cinemas, amplified to nightmare proportions, so in the end I had a few singing lessons. And then I realised I could do it. The point is, it's not a Disney animation. The producers wanted the reality with all its imperfections.'

And the reality of her singing voice, with the songs 'Fairy Godmother Song' as well as 'I Need A Hero', which Jennifer sang beautifully at the end of *Shrek 2*, proved to be first rate. In fact, the entire exercise, for her, was a fantastic learning curve. And a confidence-booster.

'I actually learned a lot about myself. I learned that with a bit of effort, I can do things a lot better than I think.'

On the home front, too, starring in *Shrek 2* had its benefits.

'The girls love *Ab Fab* but their only ever comment to me about the series is: "Why are you smoking?" That's all I ever get,' she told the *London Evening Standard*. 'This is definitely the project that has made me go up in the estimation of my children. Not because it's a chance to be part of one of the best animated films ever or because it's the start of a major Hollywood career for their mother. No. It's the fact that the film also stars Cameron Diaz.'

At the time, Diaz was involved with teen idol Justin Timberlake, so the girls were hoping they might get to meet him at some point.

'I have, of course, pointed out that he may be busy touring, singing or just generally being Justin Timberlake. That is a small fly in the ointment. But they are all clinging like limpets to the chance that it may happen.'

Shrek 2 was a huge success, breaking all box-office records in the US and the UK. (Jennifer went on to win an American People's Choice Award in 2005 as Best Movie Villain.) The movie received a 10-minute standing ovation at its Cannes Film Festival premiere in May 2004 – the first animated film to be shown at Cannes for 50 years. And Jennifer finally met up with her fellow *Shrek 2* actors. (Justin Timberlake was amongst the assembled star line-up. And the girls *did* get to meet him.)

Eddie Murphy, Cameron Diaz, Angelina Jolie, Jack Black, Will Smith and Julie Andrews were amongst the many glitterati strutting their stuff on the red carpet at Cannes. For someone who prefers to lead an outdoor or country life – in riding gear, or warm, baggy jumpers and comfy trousers paired with sturdy boots – dressing up for one of the world's most glamorous movie events was bound to be a bit of a headache.

'I had millions of people asking me: "What are you wearing?" "Are you going to get a St Tropez [fake tan]?" "Are you going to get a full body wax?" All these ridiculous questions,' Jennifer recalled to the *Mail on Sunday* at the time. 'In the good old days, you could turn up in a reasonably smart outfit or even a pair of jeans and no one would take a blind bit of notice. Now it's every inch of flesh on show, a very small bit of spangly fabric, a few ribbons and the prospect of appearing in a celebrity magazine under "worst dressed".

'I've got no fears about dying but I don't want to die of stress and the idea of all this pressure about what clothes to wear does my head in. It's insanity,' she revealed.

Unlike Patsy or Edina, the thought of going down the usual celebrity route and borrowing outfits from top designers held zero appeal for Jennifer.

'I'd far rather buy my own clothes. There's no such thing

as a free lunch. You borrow a dress from one designer then they start sending you a pair of shoes with an invite to the staff party. You can't say no and you then have to wear the shoes and find something to go with them. Then it's a free skirt and an invite to a shop opening. The whole thing is just a stress-fest.'

For Jennifer, who chose mostly plain black for the Cannes trip, the chance to observe, rather than socialise, would have been far more welcome, much better than taking her place before the world's photographers in the annual all-star Cannes line-up.

'I'd much rather have sat there and just been a fly on the wall instead of having to smile at people. I'd rather have been a waitress. Just gone round and stared at people. That's what I like doing. I wouldn't care if I never met them.'

But keeping their daughters – now aged 18, 17 and 14 – away from the celebrity family syndrome did not, in any way, prevent the Edmondson girls from inheriting their parents' creative genes. Far from it.

Ella started writing her own songs around age 10 and was, by now, planning to become a singer-songwriter. Her sister Beattie was already drawn towards acting. Freya, the youngest, was artistically inclined.

'They've absolutely gravitated towards the arts; they're very musical, they're A-star drama, music, English. I keep trying to intervene: "Are you sure you want to drop chemistry?" Because I'm still thinking, you're going to need your biology, chemistry, physics. You can't just drop biology! It's so useful. I grew up with a mother who, every time she saw something, would say: "I'm going to look that up." And I've become that person – I've become the reference book person.'

However, if her daughters did eventually wind up working as performers or entertainers, Jennifer would be unlikely to want to stop them.

'Well, it's perfectly natural, I suppose. I remember when my eldest, Ella, was about 16, she said: "If I ever work in an office, will you shoot me?"

'I think it dawned on her that me and Ade, we don't have normal hours, we're at home an awful lot compared to other parents. She realised: "What? People go to work the whole time? And then they have limited holiday periods? Shoot me!"'

By now, of course, the Edmondson girls were at the stage where parental influence was waning.

'There is a distancing,' Ade admitted. 'I spend all day trying to make them laugh and they say: "Yeah, very funny, father."

'We're quite annoying parents. We pretend to know everything that is happening in youth culture. Jennifer still pretends to know about pop music. It can look a bit tragic sometimes.'

Shrek 2 was premiered in London in June 2004, and Ade, Freya and Beattie posed happily for the cameras with Jennifer. The following month, Jennifer and Dawn were scheduled to start recording the new *French and Saunders* series. It would be their first new series for eight years, so there was considerable speculation about what the show would offer.

'We're trying to move away from parodies but the BBC love them,' said Jennifer, who freely admitted at the time that several script deadlines had been and gone without much material being produced. The creative process was desperately, some would say terrifyingly, slow this time.

'Dawn and I are the absolute worst,' Jennifer told the *Mail on Sunday* in 2004. 'We sit around talking for days on end and then all of a sudden we've got a few weeks left to put a show together. I have a panic attack when she wheels her chair round and sits next to me at the computer because I know that means we really have to do some work.

'I'm horribly lazy. I never quite believe I can do it and then when I do, I can never quite believe it's funny enough.'

This time, despite initial audiences of 6 million when the first episode of the new *French and Saunders* series went out in mid-October 2004, many critics agreed with her. The general view was that the comedy was dreary and self-obsessed.

Each new episode of the series showed the girls at work, writing their shows, developing their sketches. The movie parodies included a spoof on *Cold Mountain* with Darren Day playing the Jude Law role of Inman, Jennifer as Nicole Kidman (Ada) and Dawn in the Renée Zellweger part of Ruby.

'I found Nicole difficult because she's so porcelain-like. It's not an easy quality to show,' said Jennifer.

Guests in the series included Liza Tarbuck, Ruby Wax, Amanda Holden, Mark Lamarr, Cilla Black and the latest hot comedy duo from *Little Britain*, David Walliams and Matt Lucas.

'It seems that French and Saunders could not think of anything to put in their new series,' said the *Guardian*'s Sam Wollaston. 'So instead they came up with a brilliant plan. Let's base it around just that – us not coming up with anything for our new series. We'll make it into a parody of ourselves. We'll turn up at our office at the BBC to meet our agent and our producer and we won't have any ideas for the series. It'll be hilarious. Except it's not. Admitting that they are past it and they have comedian's block doesn't help. Nor does it get away from the fact that they are past it and have comedian's block.'

But Jennifer and Dawn's audience had not deserted them. Christmas 2004 saw their solo Christmas specials, *Ab Fab* and *The Vicar of Dibley*, reach wide audiences, yet again justifying the BBC's faith in the pair.

The *Ab Fab* Christmas special, with Eddy turning in desperation to regression therapy, netted an audience of over 6 million. As for the proliferation of increasingly negative reviews, Jennifer admitted, quite openly, in an interview with the *Mirror* that it was true: the new *French and Saunders* series didn't work. 'I think we misjudged the pace of it and how much other stuff we might need for it.

'Dawn and I enjoyed it but I think we were probably the only people who enjoyed it thoroughly because it was exactly what we wanted to do.

'I'm pretty hard on us. I think I'm probably harder than any critic and I know what is wrong. Sometimes it works, sometimes it doesn't,' she told the *Mirror*.

Times had changed a great deal since *French and Saunders* started out. Naturally, they were acutely conscious of this, she explained: 'The hard thing now is you have to make a certain programme for a certain time. In our heads we were making a late-night BBC2 show – because we always forget we've developed into mainstream now.'

However, there were hints from Jennifer, yet again, that *Ab Fab* might have finally reached its end point. 'You have a sense of when something really is past its sell-by date and it might just be now,' she said in an interview with *The Times*.

TV comedy, of course, had morphed into a harsher type of parody; the shock, 'aren't they naughty?' value of the early *French and Saunders* had gone. Audiences were now accustomed to being presented with an even more visually outrageous type of comedy and slapstick, although the soaring popularity of *Little Britain*'s Walliams and Lucas still owed much to the hilarity of some of Dawn and Jennifer's classic sketches and their parodies of the past – consider the ongoing influence of the 'Two Fat Old Men', for instance.

TV comedy shows such as the darkly sardonic *Nighty Night* (with Julia Davis), *Little Britain* and Ricky Gervais's innovative *The Office* walked away with a swathe of industry accolades at that year's British Comedy Awards on ITV on 22 December.

Yet the comedy world, in recognition of Jennifer and Dawn's influence over the years and their popularity with the general public, acknowledged their status as comedy supremos with two decades' worth of laughter behind them. The pair received a Lifetime Achievement Award for Outstanding Contribution to Comedy at the 2004 Awards – and gave their thanks in a pre-recorded clip.

Whatever her fears for *Ab Fab*'s future, Jennifer was now ready for a fresh writing challenge, a different backdrop, perhaps something more in tune with the lives of her audience, the millions of fans and admirers who had grown up with *Ab Fab* – and, of course, still wanted more Jennifer Saunders. The Big Five O was now on the horizon too, another of life's great landmarks.

A different, less frenzied type of comedy seemed to hold much more appeal now. And 2005 was shaping up as a very good time to start making it happen.

CHAPTER 7

NEW
VISTAS

The early part of 2005 saw Jennifer working away from home. In January, she went on location filming for a big ad campaign to promote Barclaycard – which had an established tradition of using well known faces, including Rowan Atkinson and Jennifer Aniston, to promote their services.

Jennifer's role in the new campaign was as a smartly dressed woman with a 'split' personality, concerned about such things as internet fraud and theft then being reassured that she need not worry – thanks to the safe haven of 'Barclaycalm'. One ad, set in Tokyo, featured Jennifer in an internet café. Another showed her in a remote part of the world being pickpocketed by a monkey on a crowded bus. (The monkey ad drew loud, angry criticism from animal charities and conservationists when it was shown that summer.)

177

In March, Jennifer and Ade continued their long-standing support for Comic Relief by participating in that year's big fundraiser. The Comic Relief Red Nose night, the all-star comic spectacular, raised £65 million. And Jennifer and Joanna happily reprised Eddy and Patsy in a hilarious *Ab Fab* sketch, joined by former Spice Girl, Emma Bunton.

Ade took part in that year's *Comic Relief Does Fame Academy* on BBC3, introducing himself by showing viewers around the sprawling Edmondson country retreat, though fans might have been disappointed that the camera hovered mostly on the sheep outside, rather than offering a decent peek at the interiors.

'He was incredibly nervous before,' said Jennifer. 'His big fear was that there would be a lot of prima donnas in *Fame Academy* and that he would get grumpy.'

In fact, at one point in the show Ade shed a few tears, much to the amazement of his wife. 'He's not like that at home. I'm the one who cries at everything on telly, anything emotional.'

Nevertheless, Ade's vocal efforts – especially his enthusiastic rendition of 'Tainted Love' – went down well and he won a respectable third place. Later, he admitted that the whole *Fame Academy* exercise had 'rejuvenated' him.

'I did the show with Edith Bowman and Reggie Yates, and I thought I was one of them; I misguidedly thought I was young. It suddenly hit me that I wasn't when they started calling me "Uncle Ade". It wasn't until later I realised that they looked at me as some kind of benign uncle, not the groovy young Turk I thought I was,' he said.

That same month, Jennifer was also filming in France,

playing an aristocratic woman in a French-language movie entitled *L'Entente Cordiale*. Jennifer played Lady Gwendoline McFarlane, the glamorous former lover of a French diplomat. John Cleese also starred in the cross-Channel action comedy, essentially the story of a French diplomat (Christian Clavier) teaming up with a sneaky interpreter (Daniel Auteuil) on a James Bond-type mission, a scenario that misfired badly on all counts: not much comedy and fairly incoherent action.

The movie, released in France in 2006, did not get a UK release and Jennifer's role was in French (with the help of some careful dubbing).

Whatever the films's shortcomings, however, she looked stunningly attractive as Lady Gwendoline. Perhaps it was the Gallic influence – working alongside a cast of good-looking and appreciative Frenchmen is hardly the assignment from hell – or just the general feel-good factor that ensues from a sojourn across the Channel. But there's no doubt she had a good time.

'It was a lovely experience,' she admitted later.

By this time, Jennifer had started working on an idea for a new sitcom. This was something she had been mulling over for quite some time. She was acutely conscious that she needed to create something different, something that was a world away from *Ab Fab*, perhaps a gentler type of comedy, and taking an early summer break in Spain was a welcome distraction. The Edmondsons joined forces with Comic Strip founder Peter Richardson and his family in a large house. This was an ideal opportunity to soak up the sun, recharge the batteries, consider her new ideas and just let her creativity 'percolate' for a while.

Holiday destinations for the family had always been chosen quite carefully, with privacy in mind. Italy has always been a favourite, but they usually avoid the better-known sightseeing or touristy spots.

'A thing you have to bear in mind if you are slightly famous and you go on holiday is to go somewhere where there aren't any British people or you get "Oh you look just like..." all the time,' explained Ade, though this kind of recognition was more uncomfortable for Jennifer than it was for her husband.

But once privacy or seclusion is guaranteed, the only way to unwind is to just indulge completely. 'The most wonderful no-exercise, drinky, eat, eat, eat, lovely holiday. Get up, sit by the pool, have giant Pimm's, then giant lunch and giant supper. There's nothing I like more in the world than that,' said Jennifer after their break.

The year 2005 was a summer of celebration, too. Just over twenty years after he'd presided as best man at Jennifer and Ade's wedding, their old friend Jools Holland was marrying his long-term partner, Christabel McEwen. So a suntanned Jennifer and a top-hatted Ade joined the 200 guests at St James Church, near Rochester, Kent, for the wedding. Afterwards they partied with the newlyweds and friends Lulu, Lenny and Dawn, Stephen Fry and many other well known names, including Ringo Starr and Mick Hucknall.

Yet while she was enjoying life, Jennifer was considering her future too. With her fiftieth birthday looming ahead in a few years, she was well aware that the course of her career was changing. She had a huge fan base and international acclaim; her daughters were growing up fast and would soon be leaving home for university, yet she couldn't just rest on her laurels and live life as a permanent Mediterranean holiday. Financially, the Edmondsons may have struck gold over the years, but the challenge of being creative, of working at what they did best, was ever present – as it is for most artists or performers, whatever the state of their bank balance.

'As you approach 50 you're tipping over the edge at the top of the hill. I'm thinking: "I've got to do everything before I'm 60." That might not be the cut-off point but I'm seeing getting towards the end now – the years go by so fast,' mused Jennifer.

Perhaps it was a combination of this kind of thinking and the need to do something lighter, less frantic than before that drew her to writing about a very different sitcom world, one involving a group of ordinary women of a certain age living in a small, close-knit English community.

The idea for Jennifer's new series came from a number of sources. First, there was the popular and successful movie *Calendar Girls*, starring Helen Mirren, Julie Walters, Celia Imrie and Penelope Wilton, a light-hearted comedy set in a small English village, where a group of Women's Institute members pose nude for a fundraising calendar – and find themselves with a sell-out success on their hands. The film had been a big hit with moviegoers on both sides of the Atlantic in 2003/04.

'I watched *Calendar Girls* and I liked the idea of all these different women meeting in the village hall and the comedy that could come from that,' said Jennifer. 'It was time for something new. There's only so many times you can have characters falling over drunk when they get out of a taxi!'

There was also an auspicious meeting with someone whose work Jennifer admired greatly.

At the time, Jennifer's brother, Simon, owned a pub in Chagford, near Jennifer's home in Devon. And well known actress Sue Johnston had rented out the pub, the Sandy Park, for a New Year celebration.

'I met Sue there and I told her I would really like to write something for her because I admire her so much. I think she's an incredible actress,' said Jennifer. 'That's how it began.'

The new idea became *Jam and Jerusalem*, a sitcom set in a fictional English village called Clatterford St Mary. The storyline revolved around the lives of the ladies of the local Women's Institute (called the Women's Guild in the TV series). (The rather odd title comes from a phrase commonly associated with the Women's Institute – 'it's not all jam and Jerusalem, you know' – and used in the *Calendar Girls* movie: the jam refers to one of the traditional activities of the Institute, jam making, and the well known English anthem 'Jerusalem' was traditionally sung at Women's Institute meetings.)

The BBC were quick to green-light Jennifer's new idea: a pilot episode of *Jam and Jerusalem* was scheduled to start filming in autumn 2005, in and around Dartmoor and North Tawton, a small Devon town near Exeter and just half an hour's drive from the Edmondsons' home. This time, Jennifer enlisted the help of a co-writer who had previously worked on *Ab Fab*, Abigail Wilson, and set about creating the script for the pilot.

Here was a fictional world a million miles away from the boozy, hedonistic big-city world of Patsy and Edina: small-town life, a close-knit community, people popping in and out of each other's homes and lives, supporting each other through life's adversities, baking cakes, enjoying cookery, the great outdoors. It was a close-up of the country life that Jennifer loved – and whose virtues she frequently extolled to the wider world.

'The community in which my mother lives is not unlike Clatterford,' said Jennifer in an interview with *Hello!* magazine in 2008. 'It has its support groups, organisations through which people can meet other people, and that – providing a support network for the people who live in the town – is basically what the Guild does in *Jam and Jerusalem*.

'The series may in part be a comedy. But the kind of organisation at the heart of it does play a vital role, especially in rural communities,' she revealed.

In the autumn of 2005, when work commenced on the pilot of *Jam and Jerusalem* and the streets of North Tawton were sealed off for 10 days of BBC filming, the recreation of fictional village life was underway.

Residents of North Tawton – including a small group of women from the North Tawton Women's Institute – mingled with cast and crew as the pilot was filmed, bringing to life Jennifer's 'dramedy' of Clatterford's small community and the day-to-day dramas – and comic moments – of the locals' lives.

Much-loved actress Sue Johnston led the cast as Sal, a down-to-earth housewife and nurse working at the local community health centre alongside her best friend, farmer's wife Tip (Pauline McLynn).

When Sal's GP husband dies suddenly after a heart attack, she reluctantly joins Clatterford ladies' group. As she adapts to all the changes in her life, she becomes much more involved with the group – and with the very diverse group of individuals within it.

'I wrote it after my dad died,' said Jennifer after the series was aired. 'It's about someone left on their own and grieving. But I wanted to show life in the country can be totally real. I really feel in Devon it's not about who you know, it's about what you do.'

Dawn French plays Rosie, who works in the local cheese factory and has an extremely odd mental health disorder. Joanna Lumley is unrecognisable as Delilah, the oldest woman in the village, and Jennifer plays Caroline, a well-to-do, horse-riding country wife. (She dines with Madonna and one of her four children is a rock star.)

Comic talents Sally Phillips, David Mitchell and Maggie Steed are also cast as village locals – and all three of Jennifer's daughters appear briefly in the series: Beattie and Freya playing Caroline's daughters; Ella, now an emerging singer-songwriter, in a cameo appearance singing 'Breathe'. Jennifer's brother Simon also has a brief appearance in *Jam* – as a pub landlord, his real job at the time.

Jennifer admitted that her daughters were roped into *Jam* to give them 'a little experience of it'.

'Freya's pretty blasé about the whole thing. Fortunately,

that makes her perfect for the part she plays. She's got to act like she doesn't care – and she really doesn't care!'

At this point, Beattie was poised to study drama at university. Ella had been immersed in music since childhood so a musical career was underway – she had initially been drawn to acting but wasn't sure she had the talent. Was Jennifer entirely happy with the idea of her daughters following the family tradition?

'If that was what they really wanted to do with their lives, I'd be cool about it,' Jennifer told *Hello!* magazine in 2008. 'But I think it would be useful to be good at lots of things, to perhaps be good at writing too, so there was something to fall back on if the acting work dried up.

'Acting can be hard,' she said. 'There can be long periods of unemployment and you need a backup plan; you've got to keep your options open.'

As 2005 drew to a close, Jennifer's own options were piling up. The pilot episode of *Jam and Jerusalem* had easily convinced the BBC to commission the first series, due to be filmed in Devon in 2006. The Christmas special of *French and Saunders* was getting underway and the challenge of writing a new series like *Jam* had given Jennifer a burst of renewed enthusiasm. A lot of it, she admitted afterwards, was because her daughters had now grown up and she had more free time. And much of her former diffidence or insecurity about her talents had been left behind.

'I have so much more time – so I got a huge burst of wanting to do things in my career,' she recalled in an interview with *Woman and Home* magazine in 2007. 'You reach a point where you realise your capabilities.

You go through life feeling you don't know quite as much as other people, then you get to a certain age and think: "Actually, I do! I probably know more." So you start driving yourself to do stuff. I don't care so much what people think of me. I'm not so self-conscious. But I'm not so tolerant, either.'

The French and Saunders Celebrity Christmas Special, shown on BBC1 on 27 December 2005, drew an audience of 6.5 million viewers. It featured a series of spoofs, including broadcaster John Humphrys in a rather odd *Mastermind* send-up, plus a sketch on the set of *EastEnders* with Shane Richie, Kacey Ainsworth and Jessie Wallace. Jennifer and Dawn were obviously keen to get close to their favourite television soap by dressing as old ladies wandering onto the set.

'I don't think I've ever been so excited or star-struck,' said Jennifer. 'I found myself going: "That's where Den was buried!" "There's Arthur's bench!" "Oh my God, there's Kat!"'

However, the show drew a shaky critical response – 'Outgunned in the comedy stakes by the average edition of *Newsnight*,' said the *Daily Telegraph*.

Yet there was one guest appearance on the celebrity Christmas special, from clinical psychologist Tanya Byron (analysing, as herself, the motivation behind the duo's immature behaviour with a stark diagnosis: 'extreme attention seeking') that marked the beginning of a new and important friendship between Jennifer and Tanya. And the consequence of this friendship would prove, in time, to be Jennifer's next major project.

This new idea was born out of Jennifer and Dawn's total fascination with a BBC3 series, a psychology driven reality TV programme called *The House of Tiny Tearaways*, which had started in the spring of 2005.

The House of Tiny Tearaways was an unusual reality programme, where a toddler sanctuary was created for families of small children. Parents at the end of their tether sought professional advice and guidance from clinical psychologist Dr Tanya Byron. Presented by Claudia Winkleman and covering a wide range of kiddy behavioural problems and scenarios, both Jennifer and Dawn became hooked on the show.

Each week, they'd eagerly discuss the previous night's episode. To the extent that they became, as Jennifer put it: 'slightly creepy, obsessive fans' fixated on the show and what it revealed about human behaviour. So they decided to invite Tanya Byron onto their Christmas special.

You might expect them to be blasé about their guests, given the long roll call of big names who had been invited to join them on *French and Saunders*. Yet Jennifer and Dawn later confessed that they were worried that Tanya would not be interested in their invitation.

'We honestly didn't think she'd do it because she looked like she had too much credibility and integrity,' recalled Jennifer in an interview with the *Independent* in September 2007. 'Luckily, she hadn't. So when we first met, Dawn and I were very nervous because we hadn't really written the sketch properly and now someone clever was arriving, who would think we were idiots. But she was great at not being panicked by lack of material. And easy to work with, fantastic.'

That first meeting with Tanya made a distinct impression on Jennifer.

'She knows how to take the piss out of me, which I respect. I was moaning about my kids, saying they treat me like a child. And she just said: "Well, stop behaving like one." I loved that she didn't let you get away with stuff.'

For her part, Tanya Byron was equally apprehensive about meeting two of Britain's best-loved female comedy performers. 'I don't often get anxious but with Jennifer and Dawn, when they asked me to do their Christmas special, I was meeting two women whom we had discussed as models of female empowerment in my women's group at university,' she said in an interview with the *Independent* in September 2007.

'What I remember is that they are quite short whereas I am quite tall and here were these two short people coming towards me, saying: "Oh my gosh, it's Dr Tanya Byron."'

By the beginning of 2006, the women began to meet up socially. Jennifer, now fully immersed in writing *Jam and Jerusalem*, sought Tanya's advice about an elderly character she wanted to write into the show. Over a long and very enjoyable dinner in London's swish Wolseley restaurant, the pair talked at length about all sorts of things. And a real friendship was formed.

At the time, Jennifer and Ade were already contemplating the changes to their way of life. Empty nesting was becoming a reality. Beattie was heading up to Manchester University to start her drama degree, the same drama course her father had followed. Ella was pursuing her musical career and leaving home. Freya wouldn't be too far behind them. And Ade, who had been toying with an idea for a sitcom about a middle-aged divorced dad moving in with his teenage kids for quite some time, found himself going through a period of gloomy introspection.

Always prone to bouts of 'shutting down' since university days, he admitted afterwards that he had gone through an especially difficult time in 2006. It followed a certain pattern.

'I just turn off, go quiet for about a week. I don't answer the phone,' he told the *Daily Mail*. 'I know it's a complete nightmare to be around me. Jennifer knows there's no jollying to be done, no "come on, cheer up". No one can get me out of it but I'm aware that she's aware and that helps.

'She's ready for when I'm finished, sort of waiting at the other end.'

But this time, it was really bad.

'I was struggling. It was about historical family stuff and I suppose the medical profession would call it depression. I prefer to call it "being unhappy" – it doesn't sound as serious,' he revealed in *Reader's Digest* in 2012.

'I asked a psychologist I knew personally if it was worth me seeing someone. They said you should never really seek help unless you're completely unable to get out of bed and go to work – that if you start down the road of analysis and drugs you're probably going to make more problems for yourself.'

So how did he overcome it all? Quite simply, he focused hard on being happy. 'I tricked myself into not being gloomy. And it worked. I'm not saying it would work for everyone, I'm not saying analysis and drugs are rubbish. I just took all the negative crap and pushed it to one side,' he revealed in *Reader's Digest*.

Two years later, after he had written and starred in the ITV sitcom he had been mulling over, called *Teenage Kicks*, Ade hinted that the bleak time of that bad year, when the two eldest had gone and he had been plunged into gloom, had not permanently affected the couple's relationship.

'In showbiz terms, staying married to someone for over two decades is a bit of a record. And maybe we're still together because we're very tolerant.

'Being a father is the most important thing I've done. It's been my life's work. There's nothing better than picking them up from the school bus, bringing them home, giving them a cup of tea, sitting around the table talking nonsense about what happened that day. Then it's gone forever, the joy of being around them.

'When they left it felt just like bereavement. I'm not sure how we got through it, except we seemed to take on an awful lot of work.'

Jennifer has not spoken openly like this about this period of their lives. It would be out of character for her to do so. But she and Ade had always made it known in interviews that family life meant everything to them, so dealing with the 'empty nest' situation would have left them both profoundly feeling the change, although they may have had different ways of dealing with it. When a change such as your children finally leaving home comes, yes, it's an inevitable moment. But it's not always easy to shift gears overnight, no matter where you are in life.

One evening, as Jennifer and Tanya were having dinner

together, Tanya mentioned an idea she had had for a television series, a character she thought Jennifer might even want to play. It was an idea she had been thinking about for some time; she had even written about it, seeing its potential as a work of fiction based on real life.

The idea was about a daytime confessional TV talk show, along the lines of the popular US chat shows hosted by Ricki Lake, Jerry Springer or Oprah Winfrey. These shows revolve around a well known host talking to people in crisis, usually with complex personal or family problems – yet prepared to reveal their woes and torment for the television cameras – and in front of a noisy, reactive live audience.

As a psychology professional, Tanya had become aware that, while the shows had considerable audience impact, there was a very obvious moral question mark over the way in which they paraded human frailties and, in some cases, misery and despair.

'A friend of mine had horrendous postnatal depression and committed suicide when the baby was quite young,' recalled Tanya in an interview with the *Guardian*. Afterwards, she happened to catch a daytime talk show about postnatal depression. 'And the host, who had clearly never talked to a child in her life, was doing a lot of fake empathy,' she added. 'I looked at the way these weeping mothers were paraded on telly and this kind of pseudo-concern flashing across the face of this highly styled chat-show host and I just remember thinking how it was all so exploitative.

'So I wrote this story about this woman who was screwed

up, probably more than the people she was interviewing on the telly.'

The idea of a TV show centred around a larger-than-life fictional character who defined the modern obsession with pop psychology and voyeurism appealed a great deal to Jennifer. Always at the cutting edge of the zeitgeist, she immediately sensed its audience potential.

'Normally, you'd say: "Thank you, send it to my agent." But I read it and thought it had possibilities. The daytime chat-show host, the person who wants to be Oprah Winfrey, was an area no one had covered. And Tanya had written it from something that angered her. That's always a good place to start.'

With her forensic eye and insightful way of analysing other people's behaviour, Jennifer found the concept of *Tiny Tearaways* and Tanya's work a compelling source of inspiration. It fitted with her lifelong fascination with human behaviour.

'I'm obsessed with the idea of why characters do the things they do,' she admitted to the *Guardian*. Though she wasn't too sure about the idea of a personal appearance on a popular reality TV show like *I'm a Celebrity ... Get Me Out of Here*.

'I would so not like to sit around the campfire with people I hardly know,' she confessed to *Good Housekeeping* in September 2007. 'But you do find yourself thinking – and this is how people fall into the trap – "I am quite an interesting person and I wouldn't be like the others. And I'd get a tan and look good." And then you remember how some people look when waking up and you think,

"That would be me". I'd come out of there wanting a facelift and Botox and everything.'

As for this positive reception to her idea, Byron, for her part, was initially stunned at her somewhat bold presumption that Jennifer might take her idea seriously.

'When I went home I said to my husband: "I can't believe that I, who cannot tell a joke without sending people into a coma, have pitched an idea to Britain's most talented comedy writer."'

The pitch was successful. 'We should do something with this,' Jennifer told her friend. The BBC agreed. Tanya Byron would be Jennifer's co-writer on the series. And so was born *The Life and Times of Vivienne Vyle*, a dark look at the world of daytime television and Vivienne, a hugely driven chat-show host.

With two major projects now on her schedule to write and film, 2006 proved to be a hectic year for Jennifer. She spent most of the later months filming *Jam and Jerusalem* in Devon. As a result, her participation in that year's *Secret Policeman's Ball* fundraiser for Amnesty International, shown on Channel 4 at the end of October, was limited to voicing some of the show's animations. Yet by year's end, when the first of six episodes of *Jam and Jerusalem* went out on BBC1 in late November, to be followed by a 40-minute Christmas special episode of *Jam* on 30 December, it was a very relaxed Jennifer who appeared on *The New Paul O'Grady Show* on Channel 4 in December 2006 to promote her new series.

'We just had a ball,' she said of making the first series. 'All those girls down in Devon, staying in a pub, what more do you want? It was late nights and a lot of drinking.'

'It's about how a community works,' she told O'Grady. 'I was fed up with how the country is represented on telly, slightly sinister, people from town moving there and finding it a bit evil. It doesn't seem like that to me.'

She admitted that the shift of focus, away from the urban, media-obsessed *Ab Fab* world, was a certain mirror of her own life in the country, where life was so different.

'There's so much media now. When we first did *Ab Fab* there wasn't the same celebrity culture. There was only *Hello!* magazine. So where I thought there was a gap, it was something that was basically about nice people. The only thing it challenges is other people's cynicism,' she told her host.

Nearly 7 million viewers tuned for the first episode of *Jam and Jerusalem*, though this dropped to under 5 million by the screening of the Christmas special. The critics weren't overenthusiastic. Many felt it was a waste of an all-star talented cast.

'*Ab Fab* seems a long time ago,' sighed the *Sunday Mirror*.

'Perhaps because of the huge cast and the way slapstick comedy runs along sadness, this first episode feels like a patchwork quilt knocked up from leftover wool. But it might be worth giving it a chance to find its feet,' said the *Mirror*.

And the ratings were good enough for that chance: a second series of *Jam and Jerusalem* was commissioned for the New Year.

By January 2007, Jennifer was looking at a series of big landmarks ahead. French and Saunders were due to celebrate their 20-year relationship with the BBC that autumn. Incredibly, it was coming up to 30 years since their auspicious first meeting at Central's movement class.

Dawn, who had recently had a huge hit of her own with *The Vicar of Dibley*, would be turning 50 that October – Jennifer's fiftieth would come the following year. The idea of a really big *French and Saunders* swansong live tour, across the UK and overseas, was already being mooted for 2008. And Jennifer was deeply immersed in writing *Vivienne Vyle* with Tanya and working on the second series of *Jam and Jerusalem*.

Both Jennifer and Ade now found themselves looking at a number of working commitments. Ade too had several projects on the go. These included a trip to Africa in February for Comic Relief, his sitcom, *Teenage Kicks*, now scheduled for a pilot episode for ITV, with a radio version going out on BBC Radio 2, as well as an ongoing television role (as consultant Dr Abra Durant) in BBC's *Holby City*.

In terms of logistics, while holiday times could still mean enjoying Chagford and the countryside, work commitments increasingly meant both being away from home a lot of the time. Or up in London more than ever.

After much thought and in the interests of work life balance, the Edmondsons decided they would move back to London and buy a new home there. At one point they had considered the idea of buying a bigger home in Devon, but all the signs were that a return to London full-time was much more practical.

'We moved down there on a whim and came back on a whim,' said Ade of their decision. 'We were planning to move to a bigger place, up the road. That made us think we were going to end up in this huge mausoleum, just the two of us – and one of us was always going to be in town. We decided no.'

'We went to Devon for the kids,' explained Jennifer. 'And it was a great thing to do because it gave me time to think about what to do next. But Ade was working too and we realised we weren't going to see each other, so we moved back to town. We've still got the house there [in Devon]. We just used to use it for holidays and then we swapped, and we'll probably swap back again.'

Creating *Vivienne Vyle* with Tanya meant researching daytime TV and watching US shows, such as Jerry Springer and the UK's *The Jeremy Kyle Show* (shown on ITV since 1996 and still being screened in 2012), and *Trisha* (1998 to 2005), hosted by Trisha Goddard, a UK version of *Jerry Springer* but without the fistfights or audience heckling of guests.

The shock value of shows such as these was, decided Jennifer, all too obvious. 'There is so much material for comedy in these shows but there were a few we watched when we thought: "This is really wrong,"' Jennifer told the *Saturday Express* magazine before the show went out on air that autumn. 'There were some people who were so vulnerable, depressed, drunk or off their heads on drugs that sometimes it made it really difficult to watch.

'It's hard to tell why people want to share their problems on these kinds of shows because when some of them come out, they look totally lost, and that's when I worry for them.'

Nevertheless, the psychology of what sort of person

becomes a talk-show host was endlessly fascinating for Jennifer. For years, she and Dawn had skilfully lampooned the successful, the famous – and their foibles. *Vivienne Vyle* meant taking all this a step further – getting right under the skin of Vivienne, a fictional TV character who was presenting the problems or dilemmas of other people to the world in order to make her own way into the hall of fame.

'They're very bright people who know what they're doing and know how to get the reaction they want,' said Jennifer of such TV talk-show personalities in the *Saturday Express*. 'But they're stuck with a dilemma. How far can they morally go and how far can they push the boundaries of taste in order to make a name for themselves? They have to find that balance between tunnel-vision ambition and what they are allowed to get away with.

'That's Vivienne Vyle's thing. She knows she's making a freak show and if people want to make fools of themselves she doesn't care. So long as it moves her career onwards, out of daytime and into prime-time TV, that's all she cares about.'

Collaborating with Tanya worked really well.

'When we started writing, Tanya wanted it to be very serious and dark. I was just cracking jokes. By the end, we'd swapped places,' said Jennifer to the *Saturday Express*. 'Often Tanya would write some dialogue and then I would look at structuring it. It's kind of like how I work with Dawn – she'll come in with loads of stuff and I'm good at shuffling it about and putting it into little packages.

'Tanya instinctively sees through people, which is spooky when you first meet her. It makes her great to write with.'

The Life and Times of Vivienne Vyle is a stark look at

the on-screen and private life of TV host Vivienne, a former weather girl. In many ways the show defines the time it is set in – the noughties – and television's preoccupation with closely examining other people's personal problems and dilemmas.

The story follows Vivienne trying to balance fame and her own insecure life, chasing the big ratings enjoyed by her rival, Chris Connor (Brian Conley). The show's producer Helena (Miranda Richardson) is a deranged and hyperactive amoral women, whose two-year-old can only speak the Spanish she's learned from her nanny because her overambitious mother is never around. Vivienne has a gay, karaoke-loving husband (Conleth Hill) and a transsexual PR adviser (Chris Ryan), and while the TV show's psychotherapist (Jason Watkins) initially insists that the guests are too mentally unstable to appear on the programme, eventually he too becomes consumed by ambition: he wants his own show.

The sleazier or nastier the stories of the guests, the more the production team tries to push the envelope for an extreme reaction. At one point, Vivienne gets beaten up by a studio guest. This boosts the programme's ratings. So the show goes more downmarket. With her insider's view of the nature of programme-making, it's clear why Jennifer was drawn to this idea.

'I have seen these people working in television,' she admitted. 'That manic energy. They learned it on coke and they can't leave it behind. Everything's going to fall down unless they're that manic. It's very different from what I've done before.'

Afterwards, Jennifer said she found playing the power-dressed, outwardly controlled woman quite exhilarating. 'I loved doing it. As soon as I walked on, something clicked. I wasn't sure how I was going to play the part. But you realise you're in complete control and it's quite a buzz. When you come off, you're still buzzing. You could walk down that corridor and just fire someone!'

Vivienne is totally devoid of endearing qualities. At one point her damaged guests are told, 'You disgust me and most of my audience', before she flounces off to have dinner at a posh restaurant.

'She is absolutely horrible,' said Jennifer. 'It's a black comedy and her ambition will cut through anything. It's nice to play someone who doesn't give a shit about anybody else. She doesn't have to love or relate to anyone, just use them. She doesn't care about her guests.'

As an actor, there was satisfaction, too, for Jennifer in the sheer contrast between her two new characters, one hell bent on cracking the harsh, ruthless world of daytime television, the other living a gentler, well-heeled, if not always smooth existence in rural England. This appealed very much to the chameleon in her own nature.

'Viv is all about control,' she said. 'I'm happy switching from one to the other.'

In March 2007, *Jam and Jerusalem*, renamed *Clatterford*, was launched by BBC America, which had co-produced both *Jam* and *Vivienne Vyle*.

As in the UK, American reviews of *Clatterford* were mixed. The blend of drama and comedy left reviewers somewhat bemused. *The New York Times* said: 'Ms Saunders goes after a centuries-old ideal: the English village. She doesn't so much mock the pastoral as bring it, complete with hymnal covers and harvest festivals, into the twenty-first century. This series takes away one vision of country life and gives us something slightly deeper.'

In June 2007, Jennifer and Dawn returned to the BBC studios to record new material for their retrospective twentieth-anniversary series, *A Bucket o' French and Saunders*. And the following month, Jennifer and Ade joined Brian May and Yusuf Islam (Cat Stevens) at a graduation ceremony at Exeter University, where they received honorary degrees for being 'leaders in their field and people the University is proud to have an association with', as Exeter's Chancellor (and former *Playschool* presenter) Floella Benjamin told the enthusiastic audience of 3,000 graduating students.

At the graduation, Jennifer and Ade were awarded honorary Doctorates of Literature. Before the event – and her entertaining acceptance speech – Jennifer admitted she was excited – and nervous. 'It's appearing as yourself that is the most nerve-wracking thing that I really don't do an awful lot of – I certainly don't make speeches, ever,' she said. 'I'm terribly intimidated by educational places, professorships, chancellors and all that kind of stuff. It makes my palms sweat slightly.'

She was, however, much happier about a visit to Manchester University to watch her daughter Beattie performing in a student comedy night. 'It was so good. And it wasn't laughter out of relief. I thought "Hurrah! She's inherited the funny gene."'

That autumn, Jennifer was starting to film the second series of *Jam and Jerusalem* in Devon. The shooting schedule was tight. 'It's a very quick turnover. But if a problem comes up in a scene, we will sit down and change it over the lunch hour,' she explained. Around the same time, *A Bucket o' French and Saunders* went out on BBC1, from 7 September to 5 October.

The retrospective, which combined classic sketches and new material and celebrated their twentieth anniversary on the BBC, was billed as a farewell tribute to the two women's work and their relationship. Joanna Lumley introduced the classics, telling viewers they would watch the duo 'get fatter and older in front of your very eyes'. But despite new spoofs on Gordon Ramsay, Simon Cowell, Britney Spears and what turned out to be a tragically poignant send-up of the late Amy Winehouse, the duo's last hurrah on TV did not ignite in any way.

In fact, so disappointing were the audience figures – under 4 million – that what was to be the sixth episode of the series was removed from the schedule – and turned up as a Christmas special at the year's end.

'These are not sketches, these are passing, unformed ideas, scribbled between yawns and chocolate oranges on French's nice sofa, then covered in makeup, forced into tights and passed off as celebrity satire. It's difficult to express just how rubbish it all is,' said the *Guardian*.

'This is an odd way to celebrate what was a real classic of its time,' observed the *Mirror*. 'It's more like a mosaic than a montage – and not a very funny one at that because half the time you're not even sure what you're supposed to be laughing at.'

Jennifer insisted that negative criticism did not upset her.

'It doesn't really bother me,' she told the *Guardian*. 'You can't take negative criticism too seriously. Obviously, I take the performance seriously but you have to take everything else lightly or you'd go mad.

'You have to care about it when you're doing it but not care about it so much your life would collapse if people didn't like it,' she told the newspaper. 'If I did that, I'd be the one on the sofa saying: "I used to be so big!" "What happened?" "Where did I go wrong?" There comes a time when there's nothing more you can do. We'll find a different way for *French and Saunders* to be on TV but the sketch format is a bit tired. There are plenty of other sketch shows on. We've done it and we've done it well. There isn't enough money invested any more to do the kind of things we used to.'

In any event, with a big *French and Saunders* tour definitely lined up for 2008, this was the time to underline the fact that theirs was still very much a working relationship.

'I love the sketch format so deeply, that's why Dawn and I are touring again,' said Jennifer. 'There's something wonderful about just concentrating on getting a laugh. I like doing more serious work as I get older, but if I didn't have the opportunity to fall over from time to time, I would just die.'

This kind of resilience in the face of criticism would prove equally invaluable when *The Life and Times of Vivienne Vyle* went out as a six-part series on BBC2 in October and November 2007. It was not a resounding success, despite a great deal of positive publicity beforehand. Audience figures never went above the 1.8 million achieved for the first episode. And the critical reception was mixed, although there was praise for the performances, especially Conleth Hill and Miranda Richardson.

'This was stylish, well honed comedy with enough sharply drawn characters to ensure at least a measure of success,' said the *Daily Telegraph*.

Overall, the problem with the show was that, while the 'bear-baiting' tactics of daytime talk-show hosts were topical enough, especially in the case of Jeremy Kyle (who had recently tackled the controversial subject of paedophiles on his morning show), the extreme nature of such television shows themselves does not easily make for comedy. There just weren't enough laughs.

'How to parody that which is already beyond parody? This was the problem facing Jennifer Saunders' new comedy. Not many marks for originality,' said the *Independent*.

'You have to ride these things,' said Jennifer afterwards. 'I felt very confident doing that and I feel very confident in meetings. It sounds pathetic really but when I walk into a meeting, I think: "I'm probably older than anyone here." And I do feel I know more.'

Jennifer and Dawn turned up again on *Parkinson* in November, to promote their forthcoming tour. As usual, they admitted that the new tour was nowhere near written. Jennifer was remarkably relaxed, quite laid-back on the show. Was her previous diffidence at dealing with interviews a thing of the past?

'I used to really hate it,' she admitted. 'But it's not so bad now. I've realised you have got to work out what you are going to say before you go on. Which is a huge leap for me.'

That same month saw Jennifer guesting on BBC's ever-popular motoring show, *Top Gear*. As a self-confessed petrolhead, there were distinct childhood influences involved in her lifelong passion for cars. 'My father was a bit of a daredevil so I think I inherited my love of speed from him. My three brothers and I used to ride scrambling bikes in the field near where we lived. I've always loved the smell of an engine.'

As a 'Star in a Reasonably Priced Car' in *Top Gear* she was polled fifth fastest whizzing down the track in a Chevy Lacetti. Later, Clarkson admitted that The Stig was 'amazed' by Jennifer's and Ellen MacArthur's driving skills: 'Both super-fast and super-smooth.'

The end of the year gave the Edmondsons time to relax briefly at home in Chagford, enjoying a traditional family Christmas. 'Ade becomes Delia Smith – he's the cook, he's excellent at it. I make fires. I'm log woman and fire woman and I do the decorations, so most of my job is done by Christmas Day. Then I just have to clear up,' explained Jennifer, who had mysteriously found herself tipped as 'the next Doctor Who' in the press, a rumour that proved to be completely unfounded.

On Boxing Day, she and Freya were out on horseback, joining 300 members of the Mid Devon Hunt for the traditional Boxing Day meet. Jennifer had only recently joined the hunt but found herself caught up in the middle of a big row that erupted between animal welfare campaigners and the Mid Devon Hunt.

The League Against Cruel Sports complained that the hunt had flouted the law which banned fox hunting with hounds. Mid Devon Hunt bosses insisted this was not true, but reporters descended on Chagford for some sort of comment from Jennifer.

'I hunted as a child and started again recently,' she said. 'I don't break the law. We simply follow a scent.'

This kind of exposure – being snapped on horseback with Freya at the hunt – was hardly welcome. But Jennifer confessed, not long afterwards, that she had finally realised what it was about being well known that provoked so much interest from others.

'I'm now coming round to realising what other people do to you because you're famous. They make you a bit shiny – and I'm not shiny in day-to-day life,' she told Janet Street-Porter in an interview with *Marie Claire* magazine in 2008.

'But I'm aware you have to deal with other people thinking it's a bit shiny. When I walk down the street with my daughter, she'll say: "Do you know the reaction you get?" But I'm honestly not aware of it because it happens behind you.'

That New Year's Eve, as they celebrated the dawning of 2008 with friends and family, Jennifer and Ade must have reflected that the future looked pretty good. Their daughters had grown into beautiful and talented young women. Their own relationship was probably stronger than ever. Work was proving demanding – but nonetheless satisfying. And, with Jennifer about to embark on a very big, farewell tour with Dawn before celebrating her fiftieth birthday in July 2008, all the signs indicated more good times and laughter ahead.

Yet it would be those around her – and their love and support – that would prove more important than ever for Jennifer during the next two years. Because unexpected dark clouds were about to appear on the horizon – and life for Jennifer and her family was about to take an exceptionally difficult and emotionally demanding turn.

CHAPTER 8

GOOD TIMES,
BAD TIMES

The second series of *Jam and Jerusalem* went out on
New Year's Day 2008. Nearly 5 million viewers (4.8
million) watched the second episode – although the show's
average audience figures were close to 3 million.

With the start of the *Still Alive* UK farewell tour now
weeks away, all Jennifer's energies were directed towards
working with Dawn on the material for the big tour. And
by this time Dawn, too, had made big decisions and
changed her own living arrangements – yet in the
opposite direction.

She had opted to be based permanently in a huge house
near Fowey in Cornwall after her fiftieth birthday the year
before. (The title 'Still Alive' was ironic: it came from the
flurry of headlines that followed Dawn's announcement
that she would be moving to Devon and didn't expect to

move again – this was erroneously interpreted as warning of her imminent demise.)

Yet while they had taken opposite directions in terms of their home base, neither had any intention of slowing down after the Big Five O and were looking forward to the tour – and to continuing to work as much as possible. Dawn, after her huge success with *The Vicar of Dibley*, followed this up with her role (as lusty Caroline Arless) in the popular BBC1 costume drama *Lark Rise to Candleford*, which also went out early in 2008.

The public, of course, were delighted to see their return to live performance again after an absence of eight years. And this was billed as the last French and Saunders national tour. Forever. Just like Morecambe & Wise, Jennifer and Dawn had seamlessly slipped into 'national treasure' mode.

'Sounds far too sensible to me,' quipped Jennifer when this was mooted. 'I'd rather be a national nuisance.'

'It's a certain kind of fun you can't replicate any other way, a sort of greatest hits,' said Dawn on the eve of the tour. 'What I'm really looking forward to actually is having some time with Jen. We haven't spent much time together in the last year.'

The tour kicked off in Blackpool at the end of February, with a string of dates across the country, winding up in May. There were suggestions that *Still Alive* might extend to a final few weeks in London after this – but, initially, it was a case of seeing how well the UK tour was received before fixing the London dates.

The caution proved unnecessary. The *Still Alive* UK tour was just as successful as their previous nationwide tours, perhaps because the farewell-cum-nostalgia factor ran high but also because their more recent solo TV appearances had maintained their visibility – and kept millions of fans happy.

The TV critics had been banging on about them being 'past their sell-by date' for years. It had become a bit of a joke. Yet it really didn't make any difference what the scribblers said: together or apart, their loyal fans would come out in droves to show their undiminished love for their sketches, their childlike abandon to sheer silliness. After all, millions of people had grown up with them. Now their grandchildren were in the audience, joining in the laughter. Can any entertainer ask for more?

'This gig proved they can still spark laughs off each other,' said the Scottish *Daily Record* after their Glasgow shows in March.

'A wonderful mix of back-screen clips of their latest hits along with re-enactments of some of their classic sketches,' chorused the *Liverpool Daily Post*, the following month. 'It was clear from the outset that this duo inspired a lot of today's comedy, like *Little Britain* and *The Catherine Tate Show*.'

Exactly. But, physically, a long tour is a hard slog, despite the high-tech special effects and the teams of people involved – and even if the travelling distances between venues are not especially great. Ade, always homesick when away from Jennifer and his daughters for any length of time, was very vocal about his dislike of touring, harking back to earlier days when he went out on the road several times with Rik Mayall and the live *Bottom* road show.

'Touring is horrible. I hate it! You do 100 shows on a tour. You won't see your kids; you stay in the same room.'

This description is essentially the gritty reality of performing live. Get to the next city, stay a few nights, perform; catch some sleep, then off again to the next venue, the next dressing room. Hordes of people running around to make everything happen, certainly. But, as every live performer knows, all the frantic activity, the go-go whirl of preparation, the last-minute panics or adjustments before the audience take their seats must culminate with that briefest, heart-stopping moment when the music starts, the lights blaze – and there's nowhere else to go but on... they're waiting for you.

'It's the noise people make when you come onto the stage, the thunderous, pounding noise,' is Billy Connolly's description of that awesome moment for the top-ranking comic performer.

OK, with 30 years working together, Jennifer and Dawn had coped with it all before, dealt with those last-minute nerves in their own unique way, using their own personal language. Live performance can also be a mixture of adrenalin and fear. A buzz, certainly. But it's so much easier to handle it all when there's two of you.

'When I'm with Dawn, half the burden of the work is gone,' said Jennifer when the tour started and the two women were assuring the press that, no, this was not the end of their relationship – or the start of a future where they never worked together again.

'We're doing another *Jam and Jerusalem* so that will be the next thing. But I'm sure we will look at ideas on things we can work on together. We have a production company together, so we are always talking about ideas. As ever, you never think too far ahead,' she said in an interview with the *Nottingham Evening Post*.

'We still share a dressing room, so we can run through our lines,' Jennifer revealed to the *Mirror*. 'Most dressing rooms are shitholes so it's nice to have Dawn there. We talk about our kids an awful lot. We're never short of conversation. We can have a whole year when we don't see each other but we're not in each other's pockets and I think that's the secret.'

'When I'm with Dawn, half the burden of the work is gone. I can't see the point of the double act if you're not friends,' Jennifer told *Woman's Own* magazine. By the time the national tour had wound up, tickets went on sale for the London *Still Alive* dates at the Drury Lane Theatre, starting mid-October. By now, Jennifer and Ade's house hunting had finally borne fruit: they had bought a house in central London in Bayswater, near London's Hyde Park. Handy for Jennifer's walks amidst the greenery with her favourite pet whippet, Olive – 'seriously pampered and never puts on weight'.

The summer saw a brief respite from work. Jennifer's fiftieth birthday in July was a private, joyful celebration with close family and friends.

'I watched you at your fiftieth birthday party looking more radiant and confident than ever, basking in the love of those who care so much for you, and I was reminded in one blinding instant how lucky I am to have you,' recalled Dawn in her book, *Dear Fatty*.

In August, Jennifer and Ade went up to the Edinburgh Fringe Festival to join the audience at the Gilded Balloon as their middle daughter, Beattie, performed on stage with her all-girl comedy troupe, Lady Garden.

History was definitely repeating itself. Like both her parents, as a Manchester Uni drama student Beattie had joined forces with other like-minded talents – Hannah Dodd, Rose Johnson, Eleanor Thom, Jessica Knappett and Camille Ucan – to form Lady Garden. Ben Elton was there too, joining his old friends from The Comedy Store days to watch the troupe perform their sketches about office life and tabloid newspapers, accompanied by much laughter: a truly proud moment for the Edmondsons – and rave reviews for the troupe. Then, in September, Jennifer was a guest at her old friend Betty Jackson's twenty-fifth anniversary collection for London Fashion Week.

Seated beside the catwalk alongside All Saints' chanteuse Melanie Blatt, Jennifer waxed lyrical about Jackson's couture outfits. 'I'm always picking what I'm going to ask her to give me after the show. And you know you'll be able to wear it for 10 years, that's the other thing. It's flattering, beautiful and sexy – without really trying.'

In a sense, that sums up Jennifer's own style.

'She looked beautiful, really beautiful,' said one Fashion Week observer after the show. 'She's tiny, much smaller than you imagine when you see her on TV. She has a very immobile face, which is why she's aged so well. And she doesn't come across as a very high maintenance person – which is probably why she seems so relaxed.'

Later, Jennifer would admit that the reality of turning fifty hadn't been a major problem for her. 'Apart from the fact that there is absolutely nothing you can do about it, I did prepare myself in the year running up to this particular birthday by pretending that I was no longer in my forties,' Jennifer told *Saga* magazine in 2008. 'That way, it took the sting out of my actual fiftieth birthday.'

She believed she'd found it harder turning forty. 'Mind you, when I was young I was convinced that if you hadn't done everything you wanted to by the time you were thirty, you might as well be dead.

'I can't drink like I used to. Or rather, I can but what used to take me a night's rest to sleep off is now a recovery lasting three days. I was never particularly physical, though, so I don't miss something I never did when I was young.'

What she was aware of, however, was a slowing metabolism. 'I now have to watch my weight – that wasn't necessary before I had my children.'

Turning fifty also brought greater insight into what she had achieved thus far. 'I've been doing the same job for 30 years now, give or take, and I undeniably know a bit more,' she told *Saga* magazine. 'I've got form. I've brought up three children. Beattie would appear to have inherited the comedy gene from me and Ade.'

She admitted in the *Saga* article that she wouldn't dream of giving Beattie any advice. 'But I'm so pleased she doesn't want to be an actress. We've both told her that there are many more opportunities – and particularly for women – in comedy.'

As for acknowledging the passing of time, she pointed to Eddy and Patsy as good examples of people who simply refused to accept the ageing process.

'I loved the fact that they never even acknowledged

oldness. I wouldn't go so far as to say I respected them, but I did admire the heroic way they carried on, oblivious to their blocked arteries.'

The London *Still Alive* gigs were a sell-out that autumn, with Jennifer embarking on the chat-show circuit early in October to promote the show on *Graham Norton*.

Sharing the sofa with the lively and likeable Cyndi Lauper, a laid-back Jennifer joked that she and Dawn had got their showbiz start 'in a whorehouse', told the entertaining story about her daughter coming home from school to ask 'Are you Jennifer Saunders, 'cause people in my class say you are?', and compared notes with Cyndi on being a celebrity mum.

Like the nationwide tour, the London *Still Alive* show, which kicked off on 15 October and ran until 8 November, was very much a nostalgia trip with pre-filmed sketches on giant projectors, Jennifer in a superb Madonna spoof, the unforgettable 'birth of *Ab Fab*' sketch and, of course, the audience links and the usual personal bickering. There really wasn't much that was new.

Yet the usually sharp-tongued London-based critics gave French and Saunders their best reviews for years: the comedy world's great and good, including comic stars Jo Brand and Catherine Tate, were in the packed London audience to cheer on the women whose careers and sketches had laid the groundwork and trail-blazed for so many other female comic acts.

'Without *French and Saunders* neither [Brand nor Tate] would have found it as easy to break into the mainstream,' said the *Evening Standard*'s Bruce Dessau. 'French and

Saunders make marvellous adolescents. And perhaps that is the secret of their success. They have always had a puerile streak, underlined in a cross-dressing encore as their lecherous fat old men that was as gloriously rude as anything by *Little Britain*.'

By November, Jennifer was hard at work on the scripts for the third six-part series of *Jam and Jerusalem*, scheduled for filming the following spring. At the same time her daughter Ella, then 22, was launching her career as a singer-songwriter before going out on tour with her father, who had recently taken on the role of Ella's manager.

'He's incredibly organised; he's got a diary on his computer so he knows what everyone in the family is doing,' explained Ella in an interview with *The Sunday Times* magazine. 'My mum is the opposite, she leaves everything until the last minute. She'll be sitting in her office with the door shut, writing, but half the time she's playing solitaire. Dad is more of a worrier; I began to pick up on when he's frustrated when I was about 14. I noticed it because I'm the same. I've always been a worrier. I was an incredibly anxious child. I made a fuss when they went off to work and I wasn't happy until they were home.'

Ella was 15 when her family moved to Devon full time. 'I think my parents wanted to chill out a bit on the work front. Suddenly, they were at home with us and it was great.'

Although Jennifer has never spoken at any great length about the way she and Ade had to juggle their TV commitments with family life in the early days when the girls were very small – and they sometimes needed nannies to help them – what emerges here is a recurring theme: the couple's strong desire to live as normal a family life as possible.

The house in Devon is remote. It is not a show-off showbiz palace of excess or a 'Look, I've made it' enclave at all. Think of a comfy, middle-class, somewhat low-key, low-beamed centuries-old home in the middle of an unspoilt natural environment.

Over the years, there were constant stories in the press that rural Devon was Jennifer's means of 'hiding' from the world, that the couple moved there because they were rich and reclusive, or they had turned their backs on the entertainment world. This was not the case. The simple truth was that their much-cherished family life in a rural environment became a priority. What was important to them was to give this kind of life to their girls before they entered the wider world. Full time, not just for holidays. The sort of childhood, in fact, that Jennifer had enjoyed so much in Cheshire.

Ella has said that her dad was 'fairly strict' and Jennifer too has openly admitted that she herself was far from an overindulgent parent: 'I am incredibly strict with them. I frighten myself sometimes at how strict I am, I'm so aware of how quickly they could become spoilt,' she said when the girls were younger.

Yet only at this point, with their daughters now adults, did this slightly clearer picture emerge of her off-screen life. The oft-repeated line that family comes first is trotted out routinely to the press by virtually all well-known people in the spotlight. Sometimes it's accurate, but in many cases you would have to look hard to find any truth behind it.

For the Edmondsons, however, family has always been the real and treasured bedrock of their lives.

Also, interviewers are frequently compelled to bring up the subject of Jennifer and Ade's enduring marriage after so long together. But looking more closely at their relationship – and what lies behind Ella's comments about how different her parents are, one a laid-back, relaxed, last-minute, 'get it done by the seat of your pants' person, the other an organised worrier – indicates that the Edmondson partnership thrives mostly because they take such a different approach: one temperament helps balance out the other. And, of course, they have shared humour or the laughter gene, now passed on to Beattie, ever since the first time they met backstage in Soho, all those years ago.

There was a lot to laugh at in March 2009 when that year's Comic Relief Red Nose Day fundraiser included a 10-minute filmed tribute sketch of Jennifer and Dawn performing a highly energetic spoof on the *Mamma Mia!* movie.

Billed as their last *French and Saunders* sketch ever, it would go down in history as one of their most entertaining, with appearances from Sienna Miller, Joanna Lumley, Philip Glenister, Alan Carr and Matt Lucas.

Jennifer, of course, had spotted its send-up potential the minute she saw the movie the year before. 'All the time I watched it in the cinema I was thinking: "If I'm not wearing Meryl Streep's dungarees within a year, I'm going to have to kill myself!"' she said.

That same month, she and Dawn voiced cameo comic roles – Miss Spink and Miss Forcible, a pair of retired burlesque actresses – in the fantasy horror children's 3D

217

movie *Coraline*, which had its UK premiere later that year and turned out to be an Academy Award-nominated box-office winner.

In an interview with the *Daily Mail* in March 2009, Jennifer revealed her core philosophy about comedy: 'I believe comedy is about staying a child at heart. If you are grown-up, you can't do comedy, simple as that. What we've managed to do is just keep hold of that little bit of us that is forever 13 years old.'

Filming had already started on the third series of *Jam and Jerusalem* when the entertainment industry decided it was time to pay tribute to the 30-year French and Saunders' phenomenon at the end of April, when the pair received a BAFTA Fellowship at that year's televised British Academy Television Awards on BBC1.

Handing the award to them, Dame Helen Mirren commented: 'They have the distinction of being the first comics to utter the word "blowjob" on TV!'

Then, to a standing, cheering, prolonged ovation from their peers and looking radiantly stunning, Jennifer told the crowd: 'After 30 years, it's kind of like the cherry on the icing, on the cake.'

Just a few days later, the Edmondsons had even more cause to celebrate when Ade came in second to *Dynasty*'s Krystle (Linda Evans) in ITV's reality cooking show *Hell's Kitchen*. At the end of the show, Ella and Beattie were there, hugging their dad with sheer delight. 'We blubbed a bit 'cause we're an emotional family,' said Ade afterwards.

As Jennifer completed filming on *Jam and Jerusalem* in the spring, it was announced that she and Dawn would be taking their *Still Alive* tour to Australia that summer, a poignant echo of the start of their long history together when they had first gone on that all-important tour to the Adelaide Festival with The Comic Strip, back in 1982.

Taking their swansong live tour to the other side of the world meant performing in eight cities in six weeks, winding up the tour in Auckland, New Zealand, at the beginning of August.

Not surprisingly, given her huge fan base in the Antipodes since the *Ab Fab* days, tickets for all dates sold out immediately and extra ones had to be added. It was a tiring schedule, with huge distances between Australian cities – the distance between Perth and Sydney, for instance, is equivalent to the distance between London and Moscow – and while their gigs were now in somewhat more salubrious venues than in their Comic Strip days, it was a demanding proposition, coming on the back of what was a more or less non-stop working schedule for the past 18 months for Jennifer – a schedule that had already included several weeks on the road touring in the UK.

The Australian reviews were not especially glowing. Some critics pointed to the hugely successful *Little Britain* tour by David Walliams and Matt Lucas in 2007, claiming the *Still Alive* tour fell a great deal short of that. Nonetheless, it was generally felt that the farewell tour was a fitting homage to the two women's talents.

'Few actresses in their fifties could swing from playing two misguided 15-year-olds discussing sex to grannies on motorised scooters, ageing Britons living large in Florida and the poignant private-school boarders contemplating

Christmas alone,' said the *Sydney Morning Herald*. 'French and Saunders say they're bowing out because such comedy is a young person's game. The pressure to create perfect, catchphrase-inducing, high-ratings comedy now could never foster such potent, pioneering and enduring silliness.'

Jennifer hadn't been back from Australia for very long before the first episode of the third series of *Jam and Jerusalem* went out on BBC2 on 9 August. This time *Jam* was aired weekly in three one-hour episodes, each one averaging just under 4 million viewers. The critics were starting to like it.

'*Jam and Jerusalem* has improved out of all recognition,' said *The Times*. 'In a gentle, Sunday night way, it's truthful and funny.'

The one-hour slot was much better suited to the programme's emphasis on drama. Many critics applauded Jennifer's performance as Caroline, struggling to come to terms with her son being posted to Afghanistan, a topical touch that was both poignant and affecting.

Jennifer later insisted that the series appealed because it was especially appreciated by an older audience. 'Commissioners are obsessed with young people, which is funny because they don't watch telly, only old people do. People say: "Oh, telly's dead." But I think: "Hang on, I'm 51 and I still watch telly." Why should we be neglected just because we've reached a certain age?'

Yet *Jam and Jerusalem* was killed off just a couple of months later. In November, actress Pauline McLynn wrote on her blog that she had learned that the BBC had decided there would be no further series: 'It was the BBC's decision, not

Jen's – she loved writing that series as much as we loved being in it. That was one of my toppest jobs as far as I'm concerned and it breaks my heart that there will be no more.'

McLynn urged viewers and fans to lobby the BBC and express their disappointment. Dawn French was quick to express her anger too.

'It was a bit of madness for the BBC because it was the most extraordinary group of mainly women,' she told Nick Ferrari in an interview on *Classic FM*. 'It was some of Jennifer's best writing and I thought she had only just got off the runway with it.

'When Jen and I first started, if we had been judged in this harsh way, we really would not have gone further.'

Despite a 'Save *Jam and Jerusalem*' petition and many angry requests to the Corporation to reconsider their decision, by the beginning of 2010 the BBC confirmed their decision: they would not commission any further series of the show. It was something of a surprise that despite the good ratings, the decision-makers had canned the series.

Jennifer did not make her feelings or views known widely. There were no raised eyebrows at this; after all, it wasn't at all unusual for her to stay silent until there was a need to step into the limelight. But this time, she had every reason to withdraw from the public gaze. Because in October, she had received some very bad news, news that put the axing of a television series into perspective.

She had been diagnosed with breast cancer.

There would be months of treatment ahead of her and she was assured by doctors, right from the start, that her prospects for a full recovery were very good. But at that particular point towards the end of 2009, as she came to terms with the news, it was clear that she was going to need all her strength and resilience to get through what lay ahead. With the love and support of her family, Jennifer was now facing the biggest challenge of her entire life. And so, as had always been her way, she chose to keep the world at bay while she got through it. Only close friends and family knew what was happening. Publicly, there would be total silence for several months. Her many millions of fans the world over would know nothing at all about it, until the worst was over.

Only a year or so later did any of the details emerge about the events surrounding that fateful October diagnosis. Ade was away on tour with his folk music band, The Bad Shepherds, when Jennifer phoned him. She had gone for a routine mammogram – she had missed her normal annual appointment because she had been away touring – and it had revealed a shadow on her breast. Then, after various tests, it was discovered that she had several malignant breast lumps. After a lumpectomy to remove them, an immediate course of chemotherapy was needed, followed by radiotherapy.

Fortunately, the lumps were small and the prognosis, from the start, was always that she would make a full recovery. But the treatment itself was wretched, miserable. Hooked up to drips for hours each week. Hair loss. Nausea. Ade and the girls did everything they possibly could to be supportive and positive for Jennifer, but it was an unhappy, troubled time for the family. They knew she would get through, but there were some bleak moments.

Given her history, it was natural for Jennifer to stay silent until she felt it was appropriate to let the world know what had happened. It's testament to the undying loyalty and support of all her friends that not a single whisper of her illness found its way into the press. But you can't help wondering: isn't it an added burden to be well known to millions worldwide yet find yourself suddenly dealing with serious illness?

Behavioural psychologist Jo Hemmings has worked with many TV and showbiz personalities. She says there are two different and quite extreme types of behaviour when well-known personalities face serious illness or personal tragedy.

'One is to completely shut yourself away and completely withdraw professionally, and the other – which is increasingly popular – is to be out and proud, saying "this is what is happening to me", becoming a flag-waver or fundraiser for the illness or disease.

'Someone who is more shy or reticent is going to withdraw; someone more outgoing is going to be more open about it – and get that identity going so that the public feel more empathy.'

Jennifer is, of course, the last person to use any aspect of her private life to push her career forward. She will always deploy her visibility to help fundraise or promote a good cause, and not only for Comic Relief: indeed, she has been a staunch supporter of breast cancer charities for many years, frequently joining fundraising marches to bring greater attention to the need for better research and improved treatment.

The experience of having breast cancer – or any serious

illness – is bound to be profoundly affecting on an emotional level, too.

'It makes you look at life differently; it pulls you up by your bootlaces and makes you think,' says Hemmings, who believes Jennifer has retained a very unique place in the entertainment world: her popularity remains consistent, despite her need for privacy. 'Jennifer has a very loyal fan base and a lot of fans around her own age. They identify closely with the person they admire, they're "stick with it" people. Her fan base would identify with her values. They kind of grew up with her and they're protective of her – you can't put a price on that.'

It wasn't until July 2010 that the news of Jennifer's illness became widely known to the public. As a guest at her friend Tracey Emin's forty-seventh birthday party in the South of France, she chose to abandon, for the first time, the wig and bandana she had been wearing to cover up her hair loss. And she cheerfully posed for photographs with her close-cropped hair, looking as elegant and svelte as ever.

Oddly enough, Jennifer had already been seen out and about in public in the months before the Emin party. Her hair was mostly covered by a scarf. Yet there was not a hint of speculation that anything was wrong.

In June, she had been photographed at Wimbledon with Ella, watching Roger Federer lose against Tomas Berdych. And earlier that month, she and Dawn had been honoured at the Great British Comedy Event, a fundraiser for the National Film and Television School, along with two other great TV comedy partnerships, Ian Hislop and Paul Merton (*Have I Got News for You*) and Terry Gilliam, Terry Jones and Michael Palin (*Monty Python's Flying Circus*). Jennifer and Ade were photographed at the event. Yet all the press focus was on Dawn and Lenny, who had announced the amicable end of their 25-year marriage that April.

Even when Jennifer and Dawn were spotted having a long and lively lunch together at The Ivy restaurant in London's theatreland, all eyes were focused on Dawn. Did she look upset? Was there any hint she was having a bad time? (There wasn't.) No one knew that the real, hidden story was Jennifer's brave resilience in the face of her illness. And that yet again, the pair's friendship was helping them support each other through their individual personal lows, lighting each other up with jokes and laughter.

In a way, Jennifer's fifty-second birthday in July was a double celebration. She had reached the point when the toughest part of her treatment was coming to an end and she could now start to look ahead again.

Jennifer did not make any public statements immediately after the Emin party. Her agent confirmed the news in the simplest terms: 'She has great friends and family, who have been a huge support. She's feeling well and wants to focus on the positives of this experience, rather than the negatives. She feels incredibly lucky to be alive.'

A few weeks later, there was unexpected good news when it was reported that Jennifer was starting work on writing the story for the Spice Girls' musical, *Viva Forever!*, the brainchild of Judy Craymer, producer of the *Mamma Mia!* musical.

Then, in September, Jennifer was seen with her friends Tracey Emin and Miranda Richardson at Betty Jackson's fashion show at Somerset House. The message was loud and clear: she was starting to enjoy life again and was on the road to recovery.

Further evidence of this came not long afterwards when she fired the starting gun at a fundraising event for 2,000 runners in Cambridge on behalf of Wallace Cancer Care. 'Having undergone treatment for breast cancer myself, I understand how important it is to have the kind of support Wallace Cancer Care provides,' she told the assembled crowd.

At the end of September, Jennifer and Ade watched on with pride and delight as their 24-year-old daughter Ella married her boyfriend, builder Daniel Furlong, in a church wedding near Chagford, followed by a reception for 200 people at the family home. The couple, living nearby in an old three-bedroom cottage near Okehampton that they had started renovating, were already looking ahead to starting a family – much to Jennifer and Ade's delight.

It wasn't until after Ella's wedding that Ade finally broke his silence regarding Jennifer's illness. Initially reluctant to speak about it, he decided to talk publicly because he felt that press reports had mistakenly implied that his wife's treatment had finished and the whole thing was over. No one, he said at the time, 'battled' cancer.

'It's just a long, slow, miserable grind,' Ade told the *Daily Mail*. 'The treatment lasts five years and we're only a year into it. The big chemotherapy's finished and the radiotherapy's finished. There's this low-level treatment that carries on for five years but you know from the beginning of the treatment when it's going to stop.

'I hate the word "battle". You just get battered with a

load of drugs. People want the words "trauma", "battle" and "life changing" but it's not a great three-part TV drama full of moments; it's a long grind, like a slow car crash that will last five years and then, hopefully, we'll get out.

'Something like 140 women a day learn that they've got breast cancer,' he told the interviewer. 'You don't find out the worst until they find a shadow in a picture. Then people look at it a bit more. They test it and say: "We think it's this." "We'd better do another test." They grab a bit and think it might be bad so you might have to have a bit of radiotherapy. It's all very incremental.'

The chemotherapy, he admitted, was the truly bad part: 'It knocks you out and that's just brutal. You're hooked up to drips and things for three or four hours once a week. And the hardest thing was there was nothing I could do to take the misery away from her.'

The situation was tough on everyone in the family: 'It's very hard to support someone and make them feel better through that misery. It's hard to keep them cheerful. She tried to stay positive, but it's hard to bolster someone and say "You're looking great today" when their hair's falling out. It's hard to convince them they look great, even though they do to you.

'But neither of us ever really thought death was a likely prospect. They were quite small lumps and were of a certain grade – and the prognosis was very, very good from the start. It's just that the amount of treatment grew as they found slightly different grades of this or that.

'So no, we weren't blubbing, thinking: "Oh no, she's going to die."'

They were already a close family; the illness just drew them even closer.

'I don't think we needed cancer to know we all love each other. The children have always been there but they did come round a lot more and were a great help.'

Jennifer's decision to turn up at Tracey Emin's party without a wig was, said Ade, a purely practical decision.

'She just decided it was so f***ing boring, putting a wig and hat on the whole time. And it was really, really hot. She'd also got used to what she looked like. By that time, she had some hair back and wasn't as bald as she had been,' he told the *Daily Mail*.

'It was a nice soft way for it to come out – and we were used to it by then. It's a bit like trying to get a series on the telly. By the time it gets there everyone is surprised but you've been working on this for years.'

Ella's wedding, of course, had been a wonderfully uplifting day for everyone after the miserable gloom of the previous months. 'It was the best wedding I've ever been to. My speech descended into a blubbery mess. I made myself cry and I made everybody else cry, by telling the truth in a beautiful way. There's also this idea that there might be grandchildren, which we'd like some of,' said Ade.

Jennifer's return to a normal working life was now gaining momentum. In October, BBC Radio 2 announced that French and Saunders would be presenting three end-of-year shows on Boxing Day, New Year's Day and 3 January 2011. And in November, Joanna Lumley revealed that she was talking to Jennifer about the idea of an *Ab Fab* revival.

'Jen wrote to me and said: "What do you think?" And I said bring it on – because we are all still here.'

2010 had been the worst, most difficult year of Jennifer's life, but she had come through it. As the year ended, the clouds were gradually beginning to lift. With a revival of *Ab Fab* now mooted, happier times were bound to be on the horizon. Eddy and Patsy, the Bolly Sisters, were older but no wiser – and as outrageous as they had ever been. And here they were, reckless and attention-seeking as ever – and poised to make yet another comeback.

CHAPTER 9

VIVA FOREVER!

While the nation unwound at home over the long Christmas/New Year break, Jennifer and Dawn took to the airwaves, presenting three BBC Radio 2 shows over the holiday period. And it was at this point that Jennifer spoke more openly about the events of the previous year.

'2010 – not my best year. Some misery, some uplifting moments, a bit of a learning curve and all that stuff.'

She talked about the end of her treatment for breast cancer. The chemotherapy, she said, was due to finish quite soon. 'I've got a little port here where they push the chemicals in under the skin, a little tube that goes down into your vein and that comes out in March. That's like the last sort of moment of chemicals I have to do for the old breast cancer, so that's a nice positive in March.'

There were, she admitted, certain things she would be

really glad to do in 2011. 'I'd like to see more live football, drive my car in a skid pad, probably ride my horse a bit more just in the field – with no shoes on, potter about in my garden.'

The three Radio 2 shows were warmly received and Jennifer and Dawn signed up to do a series of special Bank Holiday broadcasts each Bank Holiday weekend throughout 2011.

'We pop up on high days and holidays and we always try to get someone famous and their mum,' said Jennifer. 'The most difficult thing [about radio] is timing. Dawn can't read a clock to save her life so she often cuts off a guest five minutes too early.'

By April, the BBC confirmed that the details of the brand-new *Ab Fab* series, celebrating the twentieth anniversary of the original show and reuniting the original cast, were now in the process of being finalised. Yet although she didn't reveal anything about it until much later in the year, during the spring of 2011 Jennifer was having a brief but difficult time adjusting to her post-cancer treatment.

The chemo was over. But, as tends to be the case following breast cancer, doctors had prescribed the drug tamoxifen for her – to be taken for the next five years. (Tamoxifen is a hormone-based drug that suppresses oestrogen levels and reduces the risk of the cancer returning.)

'I found the tamoxifen the hardest thing because it changes you. It's like suddenly becoming older. You feel fagged out, you lose your motor and it makes you feel depressed. You have that "I want to go to bed and sleep forever" kind of feeling. Normally I have the energy to get up, get ready and do something, but I wasn't starting my days until 11am or 11.30am, even though I was awake.'

Her close friend psychologist Tanya Byron helped her see that this was depression. 'I'd say: "The whole world is against me, everyone else is wrong about everything." And she'd say: "No, darling, I think that might be depression."'

Eventually, Jennifer took a course of antidepressants.

'And honestly, it was like, "Give me more pills!" It was brilliant.'

She also revealed that the support she'd received from all those around her had made an enormous difference in helping her get through this difficult time.

'Ade's a sort of rock in that he never gives anything away and he's very good at letting you get on with it. I think he was very strong about that,' Jennifer told the *Mirror* in 2011. 'And the girls were brilliant. Freya was at home most of the time and was fantastic. And I have really good girlfriends who'd come and look after me and sit with me in the chemo sessions.'

But now that all this was behind her and she was starting to feel so much better, the writing of the Spice Girls' stage musical, *Viva Forever!*, was starting to preoccupy Jennifer's thoughts. It was a project she had set her heart on creating, even though she had originally heard about it when she had just embarked on her cancer treatment – an indication of how strong-minded and courageous she had been right at the very start of her illness.

'My agent, Maureen Vincent, was having a meeting with Judy Craymer, who created *Mamma Mia!* Judy started talking about a possible Spice Girls project and my name came up. I'd just begun chemo. But as soon as I was told of a possibility, I said: "Maureen, if I don't get this, I'm going to be *so* cross,"' said Jennifer in an interview with the *Daily Mail Weekend* magazine in 2012.

Jennifer didn't know Craymer at that point: 'I'd only ever sent her up rotten in the sketch Dawn and I did for Comic Relief about *Mamma Mia!* And she was so good about it. She sent me a lovely letter saying how it had made her laugh.'

The Spice Girls were fantastic. 'They pitched it just right for girls of a certain age. So I wanted to give my story that sort of spirit.'

The storyline of *Viva Forever!*, set to the music of the Spice Girls and featuring a number of their hit songs, including no. 1 hits such as 'Wannabe' and 'Spice Up Your Life', is the story of a young girl who wins a music talent contest. After leaving her family and friends behind, she finds that money and fame do not bring happiness.

'It's half dialogue and half music in a two-hour show. So I have to tell quite a complicated story interspersed with songs relevant to the action.

'The songs are remarkably good. They're generally on a theme that runs from the excitement of early success and love right through to the downside of fame and relationships.'

May brought really sad news for the Edmondsons and their friends. Composer Simon Brint, a close family friend and godfather to Ella, was dead at the age of 61. Simon had worked with Jennifer, Ade and Dawn since The Comic Strip days and had composed the music for *French and Saunders* and many other well-known TV series over the years. Only recently, he had been playing with Ade, Phill Jupitus and Neil Innes in a band called The Idiot Bastard Band.

'He did the music for all the years we've been French and Saunders; he was a musical genius. We miss him hugely. I owe him so much,' said Jennifer.

Jennifer's extensive commitment to charitable work and fundraising events for breast cancer charities was in evidence the following month when she joined the annual London MoonWalk fundraiser for breast cancer charity Walk the Walk. And in July she was awarded an honorary doctorate for services to the entertainment industry by Edge Hill University in Ormskirk, Lancashire.

Watched by an audience that included her proud mum, and in typical Jennifer style, she told the students: 'When I was told months ago about this, I thought I would prepare with diligence and intensity like you have all done for your exams. So I started it last night, with a strong coffee and a can of Red Bull. I Googled information, copied and pasted bits and changed a few words so it looked original.'

Following a July summer holiday on Italy's Amalfi coast with her family – 'the food and the weather were out of this world' – Jennifer's growing list of work commitments saw her once again starting to divide her time between her homes in Devon and London. In many ways, she reflected, life was pretty much as it had been before the breast cancer.

'I feel very positive about the future,' she told *Woman's Own* magazine in August 2011. 'Having cancer was a bit like having a job without having anything to do.'

She certainly didn't court the idea of being treated differently because of her illness. 'People have much worse times, so it would feel ghastly to want to evoke any sort of sympathy or something,' she told the *Scotsman*. 'I think I've always been a chilled person, actually, because the kids keep you pretty chilled. I'd do writing in the day and then you go home and family life would take over.'

As for work, it was very much business as usual. 'I don't really know if it has affected my outlook on work much, actually. I think what I realised was that it took me a long time to get back to where I was before I was ill. I thought I was there. But I really wasn't because you physically get tired very quickly and mentally, it takes you longer to get up to speed.'

In August, filming was scheduled to start on the new *Ab Fab* series; three new episodes had been commissioned, two to be shown on BBC1 on Christmas Day and New Year's Day, the third around the time of the London Olympic Games in summer 2012. The high expectations and the increasing hype around the comeback of Edina and Patsy after their long absence did trouble Jennifer at first.

'I worried that bringing the characters back would feel too ridiculous somehow, but luckily everyone was up for it and the next thing was to work out how the characters had moved on – or not moved on – and make sure everyone was happy with that,' she revealed to the *Scotsman*.

The girls' age, she admitted, posed the biggest challenge. 'No one ever knew when Patsy was born or how old she was. Logically, Edina was about 60 – they kind of make sense older,' Jennifer told Mark Lawson in a Radio 4 interview. 'I go back and I look at old shows because you kind of lose confidence in what it was or whether it can be funny again.'

Yet because Edina is still so much a part of Jennifer, in a way writing the characters again came quite easily, she told Mark: 'Basically, any of my neuroses that are slightly submerged are hers – but hers are bigger. Being hard on yourself is a slight thing in me – but it's massive in her. She feels that her fatness is really holding her back in life. She can never get quite beyond it.'

When *Ab Fab* was first launched 20 years before, it had coincided with a financial downturn and recession in the UK. Two decades on, the country was yet again facing the same situation.

'I thought that was quite odd,' Jennifer said in the Mark Lawson interview. 'There's something about those people [Patsy and Edina] who don't care about money that probably makes sense in a recession. Because they are much older too, they are even more desperate to get out and do things. I had to think: "What is it now?" Now there's so much stuff, crazy stuff happening, it's like Edina and Patsy have stood still, but the world's caught up.'

At the beginning of August 2011, *Laughing at the 90s*, a two-hour look at television comedy of the era, went out on Channel 4 with Jennifer as host, reflecting on the decade when *Ab Fab* first emerged and sharing anecdotes with Ade, Dawn and many of comedy's biggest names. And, at the end of the month, she and Dawn hosted their increasingly popular Radio 2 August Bank Holiday special.

This is Jinsy, a surreal eight-part comic series, went out on satellite channel Sky Atlantic in September, with Jennifer as the Voice of Miss Reason. An offbeat comedy, set on a fictional island stuck in the time warp of the 1970s, Jennifer was joined by a number of big comedy and acting names, including Simon Callow, Jane Horrocks, Harry Hill, David Tennant and Catherine Tate.

That September, she revealed to *Woman's Own* magazine that she had had a nasty accident in the summer months – and had been rushed to hospital after falling down concrete steps and splitting her head open.

'I was walking the dog around 1.30am, having had people round for supper. I'd had a little wine but not a lot. And while the dog was sniffing round a lamp post, I thought: "I'll lean back on these railings."

But a gate to someone's basement swung open and she fell backwards down two flights of concrete steps. 'I whacked my head so hard. But I didn't fall unconscious, luckily. I'm amazed I didn't die.'

Somehow, she managed to stumble home.

'When I got back, my white dress was covered in blood,' she told *Woman's Own*. 'I'd split my head open at the back and had to go to hospital to have it glued. I was alright once I'd got over the pain.'

Yet this incident proved to be a mere blip in the proceedings: very soon Jennifer was having fun again, joining forces with her old friend Peter Richardson and The Comic Strip gang for *The Comic Strip Presents'* latest 60-minute film, *The Hunt for Tony Blair*, shown on Channel 4 in October.

Shot in the style of *film noir* and penned by Richardson and Pete Richens, the outrageous spoof starred the charismatic Steven Mangan as Tony Blair, multiple killer on the run. Eventually he finds himself being seduced by Maggie Thatcher, a cameo superbly played by Jennifer in Bette Davis/*What Ever Happened To Baby Jane?* mode.

'Bonkers, but it works,' said the *Guardian* of the film, and it is probably one of Peter Richardson's most successful creations. For Jennifer's fans, it was also a fitting (brief) warm-up prior to the return of *Ab Fab*, due to be screened on Christmas Day.

She herself, however, claimed beforehand that she was mystified by the audience's continuing fascination with the show. There was, she said, no clear reason for its ongoing success.

'I have no idea why, other than the characters aren't trying to be anything they're not, and they're not politically correct. I think it's because the show is just panto,' Jennifer told the *Scotsman*. 'Its gags, the characters are larger than life, and it's not pretending to be sophisticated in any way.

'I don't think I ever had a concept of where it would go. It's extraordinary that it's still going on. Because at the time it launched there was still a sort of *Fawlty Towers*' theory, which was do two series and get out. And that was it. If you pushed for more, you were really milking it. Whereas now, nobody thinks like that. Now you're just grateful to get a programme made.'

Probably because she was so in tune with the way in which television had changed and how difficult it can be to get a comedy career off the ground, Jennifer revealed at this point that she had for many years put considerable effort into getting wider recognition for Miranda Hart.

And it eventually paid off: Hart is now one of TV's most popular comic actors/writers/performers and has her own award-winning show, *Miranda*. She was far from being an overnight success, earning her comedy stripes over many years, appearing briefly in *Ab Fab* in 2004 and subsequently in various other TV comedy series, including *Nighty Night*, *Lead Balloon* and *Not Going Out*.

'I just thought she was too funny to slip through the net,' Jennifer told the *Scotsman*. 'I could feel her slipping through the net because she wasn't getting anywhere. And she was getting frustrated.

'So I'd turn up at all her readings and meetings and clap loudly and say: "This is a very funny woman."'

In the *Scotsman* article, Jennifer revealed her disappointment at the limited opportunities for new TV talent. 'There are so many great people out there but companies only want to sign a name for their shows. Which is so dull on television. Not enough people get opportunities these days because the casting and commissioning is so narrow.'

In November, Jennifer and Ade were at the opening night of Trevor Nunn's production of *The Lion in Winter* at the Theatre Royal in London's West End, where Joanna Lumley was playing Eleanor of Aquitaine and Robert Lindsay Henry II. And at the end of the month she was on fine, super-relaxed form when she appeared again on *The Graham Norton Show*, this time talking about the return of *Ab Fab*.

'It all seemed the same except at the read-through there

was a lot of snapping open of spectacle cases and people bending low to look at the lines… and the click of bones as you walk along,' she said deadpan.

In December, Jennifer attended the annual Olympia Horse Show, the major showcase event for the British equestrian world. Her visit coincided with the news that she was the latest showjumping ambassador for UK showjumping, lending support for the sport – her childhood passion – in the run-up to the London Olympics the following year.

'I haven't been to the Horse Show since I was a teenager,' she admitted. 'But there's something so evocative about the smell – and the place.'

The *Ab Fab* Christmas specials finally returned to BBC1 on Christmas Day and New Year's Day 2012 – to a rapturous welcome. (They would also be seen in America and Australia early in 2012.) Just over 7.4 million people tuned in for the two episodes.

With Edina as much a walking disaster as ever (although Lacroix was now ditched for Stella McCartney), Patsy still pissed and pill-popping (a mere £50,000 in debt to her drug dealer) and loopy Bubble baffled as to why she was unable to write on her iPad with a felt-tip pen, it was as if they had never been away. (Inspired guest casting for Christmas Day included the star of the Danish drama *The Killing*, Sofie Gråbøl, in a hilarious dream sequence where Edina thinks she's talking in Danish.)

Critics were generous in their praise for the new show's entertainment value (although some complained that the studio audience was a bit too overenthusiastic in their prolonged response to the return of the show and the first sighting of Edina and Patsy after their long absence).

'Who else but Patsy could deliver the immortal line: "This magazine isn't aimed at normal people it's for the diamond-studded whores of the oligarchs?"' quoted *The Times*.

'Whether she was pulling spliffs out of her bun or discovering to her horror her own age, Joanna Lumley's performance was a comic wonder, a turn which in itself makes you glad you watched,' said the *Telegraph*.

'The Saunders-Lumley dynamic is still beautiful,' commented the *Guardian*. 'And they have adapted to take on the modern world. Edina's attempts to adopt modern youth speak – wa'gwan, wha'happen etc – are a special joy. Yeah, she's still got it; they both have.'

How satisfying was that? Publicly, Jennifer had always remained sanguine in the face of what had, on occasion, been a barrage of less-than-flattering write-ups of her shows. But this time, she could allow herself a moment of pride. After all she had gone through in the past 18 months, here was a unique, and very rewarding, triumph for her and everyone involved with *Ab Fab*: two decades had come and gone, and not only were the *Ab Fab* women still around, the audience loved them as much as ever.

Imperceptibly, seemingly without effort and with her typical understated flair, Jennifer's star had risen even further. 'Legend' is an oft-repeated word in show business, frequently used quite carelessly, but the fact remained that Jennifer Saunders, funny woman extraordinaire, had now achieved legendary status in the entertainment world.

Yet there was no chance she would take it all for granted.

On the BBC Radio 2 show on New Year's Day 2012, Jennifer admitted that, with all her success, she still had her moments when she experienced the perennial insecurities of showbiz, still worried that the next job or offer might not come along at all.

'The minute you think you're never going to work again, you get more work than ever. 2011 was a good year, but this year is going to be fantastic. I turned things down when the girls were growing up, but now I'm saying yes to pretty much everything.'

She wasn't exaggerating. In February, she appeared in a big advertising campaign for Choccy Philly, a mixture of Cadbury's milk chocolate and Philadelphia Light cheese spread. And, by now, the Spice Girls' musical, *Viva Forever!*, was close to being written, with anticipation increasing around the show's opening in London at the end of 2012.

'I've had 10 out of 10 for enjoyment on this project. I can't wait for the first night. All the Spice Girls will be there – they have real affection for each other and it's also clear that this was a very special time of their lives,' said Jennifer.

Former Spice Girl Melanie Chisholm said that Jennifer's input into *Viva Forever!* would make it a hugely successful musical. 'We've got quite a lot of history with Jennifer so she knows us and the dynamic and chemistry,' she told the *Newcastle Evening Chronicle*. 'It's based around the music of the Spice Girls; it's not autobiographical but I still think Jennifer having that knowledge of us has influenced her, whether it's personality traits in the characters or some of the relationships.

'From what we know about the characters and storyline and how the songs are going to be used it just has the potential to be incredible.'

Yet the big projects didn't end there. Although it had been talked about virtually since the time *Ab Fab* had first tasted success, Jennifer confirmed that *Ab Fab* the movie was also now very much on the drawing board, due to be written by the end of 2012. The setting: a yacht on the French Riviera. The quest: er... more good times, more hedonism for the world's most over-the-top pensioners.

'It's Eddy and Patsy in search of *la dolce vita*,' revealed Jennifer. 'They're looking for what they imagine a glamorous life should be: the perfect place to sit or that perfect pair of sunglasses. In the meantime they take Saffy's daughter – and then manage to lose her.'

In late March there was a brief, hilarious *Ab Fab* special spoof for sport's big fundraiser on BBC1, Sport Relief, with Edina – the planet's most unlikely gym bunny – taken through her paces by celebrity personal trainers Colin Jackson and Linford Christie, and Patsy introducing herself to Kate Moss, Stella McCartney and model David Gandy with an outrageously Patsyesque gaffe to Kate – 'Us 39ers must stick together.' The five-minute clip provoked a Twitter storm: a double whammy for Kate and *Ab Fab*'s legions of devoted followers.

By now, there were several TV projects in the pipeline. Jennifer had accepted a cameo role as a psychotic prison governor – 'a sexual Margaret Thatcher' – in a new BBC3 six-part comedy sitcom, *Dead Boss*, penned by *Pulling*'s Sharon Horgan and stand-up comic Holly Walsh.

'She's sexy. And certifiably bonkers. I order the guards to dress up in a variety of outfits so I can paint portraits of them,' said Jennifer before filming of *Dead Boss* commenced.

Jennifer also spent several weeks in April and May filming at Crom Castle in Fermanagh, Northern Ireland for her leading role in another new BBC six-part comedy series entitled *Blandings*. Set in 1929 and based on the famous P.G. Wodehouse stories, the backdrop for the series is the fictional Blandings Castle (or 'dysfunction junction'), with Timothy Spall playing the befuddled Lord Emsworth and Jennifer his sister Connie. Others in the cast include comedian actor David Walliams (in a guest appearance), *Harry Potter* actor Mark Williams and singer Paloma Faith.

The setting for the shoot at Crom Castle, in the picturesque and tranquil countryside around Lough Erne, helped make the filming of Blandings a memorable experience for Jennifer and the cast.

'Jennifer was very emotional when she left,' revealed Crom Castle's Manager, Noel Johnston, after filming ended. 'She said she had never worked in such beautiful surroundings.'

Horse riding, too, would now be revealing a very different side of Jennifer to the world: a two-part documentary for ITV called *Saunders in the Saddle* (screened in August, following the 2012 Olympics) was also filmed in the spring of 2012, with Jennifer following Olympic hopefuls Piggy French and Lauren Shannon – as well as visiting the spring horse trials at Gatcombe Park and walking the course with ex-Olympic equestrienne Princess Anne.

Her own horse riding skills were being honed by daily

training sessions. 'I want to go in confident. It's just finding enough time,' she told the *Mirror*.

In May, Jennifer joined 17,000 other women at London's Hyde Park for the annual Moonwalk fundraiser for the breast cancer charity, Walk the Walk. Smilingly flashing her bosom in a beautiful Swarovski crystal bra, alongside other well-known names, including actress Harriet Thorpe, she cheerfully completed the half marathon through central London, tweeting to her Twitter followers throughout.

'Full of energy,' she tweeted. 'Bring it on!'

On 27 May at London's Royal Festival Hall, a visibly surprised Jennifer stepped up from her seat to receive yet another award from her peers for *Ab Fab*. This time, it was a BAFTA Award for Best Female Performance in a comedy programme.

'I wasn't really expecting this,' she told the assembled showbiz luminaries, including a clearly delighted Ade.

Afterwards, in a filmed interview with Kate Thornton, Jennifer admitted she had been shocked to win, given the longevity of the series and in view of the fact that very popular comic actors – Olivia Colman, Tamsin Greig and Ruth Jones – were the other nominees.

'It's quite a strong category. Olivia, Tamsin and Ruth are completely brilliant. I felt really honoured,' said Jennifer.

And what did she plan to do with the award? 'I might make it into a small bra,' she quipped, in a nicely timed mention of her recent Moonwalk .

BAFTA awards aside, at the end of June, it was announced that the Spice Girls Musical, *Viva Forever!*, would be opening on 11 December at London's Piccadilly Theatre. Appearing alongside the Spice Girls at the official launch, a very tanned and relaxed looking Jennifer said: 'I like the songs even better now'.

During this time, *Dead Boss* went to air on BBC3 for six weeks and ran until the end of July. Reviews for the programme, which focused on a woman called Helen (played by Sharon Horgan), who had been jailed for 12 years for killing her boss, were mixed. Yet critics were unanimous in their praise for Jennifer's cameo as Margaret Brodie, governor of the prison.

'On top of the succinct characterisation and sly humour, there's a murder mystery plus a fine cameo role by Jennifer Saunders as the prison governor,' said the *Telegraph*'s Terry Ramsey. 'I really enjoyed it.'

Reviewers were not as kind when the final *Ab Fab* 20th anniversary special, this one being Olympic-themed, aired on BBC1 in late July prior to the opening of the Olympics.

The general critical view was that Eddy and Patsy were in danger of losing their edge, but the show still had some good moments. Patsy's admission that she needed Tena Ladypants for bladder weakness and her comment to Olympic guest and fashion designer Stella McCartney that she'd '*had*' Stella's dad, Beatles singer Sir Paul McCartney; 'I think it was him, it was one of the four, might have been Yoko Ono' was classic *Ab Fab* humour.

The *Telegraph* said the Olympic special 'would have won no medals for comedy'. The *Independent* agreed, calling the show 'an irrelevance'. 'Ab Fab,' said the *Independent*'s

Gerard Gilbert, was 'growing old disgracefully.' Nonetheless, over 5-million loyal *Ab Fab* fans tuned in. And, just a few days later, on the eve of the opening ceremony for the London Olympics many more fans were delighted to see Jennifer and Joanna, in Patsy and Edina mode, jogging along the streets of *Ab Fab*'s home territory, London's Kensington and Chelsea, both holding the Olympic torch aloft.

Yet if 2012 was to prove one of Jennifer's busiest and most successful years for some time, there was one more professional achievement to come that would cap it all: the chance to work with Dawn again. Dawn received much acclaim for her work with Alfred Molina in BBC2's *Roger and Val Have Just Got In*, and her guest appearance as a judge on ITV's summer reality talent show, *Superstar*, alongside the musical genius Lord Andrew Lloyd Webber and singers Melanie Chisholm and Jason Donovan, was a huge success. With more TV commitments lined up for Dawn, and a new much-awaited novel penned and scheduled for publication in the autumn of 2012, the pair were longing to work together again. The only problem was finding the time.

'At one stage, we played with the idea of co-hosting a TV chat show,' revealed Jennifer. 'We text a lot. I'm beginning to notice missing her a bit more. There are moments when I really miss doing the *French and Saunders* sketches. I'll see something like *The Iron Lady* and think: "Dammit, I wish we were still doing that."'

Cue the Comic Strip's driving force, Peter Richardson, yet again. And sure enough, Jennifer and Dawn found themselves working – and laughing – together sooner than they might have imagined. The 30th anniversary of *The Comic Strip Presents* was coming up at the end of the year and in July it was confirmed that the original Comic Strip team of Jennifer, Dawn, Ade and Peter would be reuniting once more for a new *Famous Five* adventure, 'Five Go to Rehab', another Enid Blyton-style spoof movie.

Filming of 'Rehab' took place in Dorset, the same county where it all began, all those years ago, and the girls and Ade were pictured in a break from filming, clearly having a whale of a time. Scheduled to be shown on UK comedy channel Gold in November 2012, the programme would also be accompanied by a special documentary entitled *30 Years of the Comic Strip*.

'I do get people saying, "The Comic Strip is the reason I got into comedy,"' said Richardson. He's being modest, of course. Ask any aspiring young comedy writer for their opinion of the Comic Strip and they will tell you just how inspiring Jennifer, Dawn and the gang have been to generations of comedians.

The good news extended beyond the work place for Jennifer, too. On the home front, the news that Ella was expecting her first child, due at the end of the summer, brought personal joy for the Edmondsons. Since Ella's wedding day, Jennifer had made no secret of the fact that she could hardly wait for the arrival of her first grandchild.

So, with Freya studying fashion at a London art college, and Beattie's comedy group, Lady Garden, performing sketches throughout the summer in comedian Russell Kane's comedy show, *Live at the Electric,* a late-night showcase for the next generation of comedy performers, there is no question that the Edmondson girls are now well and truly on their way to success.

Said Jennifer: 'So I have a comedian and a fashion designer. I'm sure Edina would approve!'

Wouldn't she just! Let's stop for a minute here and indulge in one of those typical *Ab Fab* fantasy sequences.

It's the first night of the musical *Viva Forever!* and Eddy and Patsy are there, overdressed and dripping with bling, hustling their way down the red carpet, through the noisy crowds of fans, the international TV crews, the click-click of hundreds of cameras, nuzzling up to the Sweetiedarling Spice Girls and the all-star gathering; trying, in true Edina style, to hog the limelight that rightfully belongs elsewhere.

Yet on the real *Viva Forever!* opening night, one of London's biggest, most hotly anticipated showbiz events of the year it is, of course, the musical's writer, Jennifer Saunders, who is sharing the limelight with the Spice Girls. She's still at the very top of her game, even after three decades in the business, still very much the self-effacing, slightly reticent woman who climbed those shadowy Soho stairs for a lark all those years ago, never dreaming in a million years that it would lead to the acclaim and worldwide popularity she enjoys today, and she's still ready to bring on more.

Jennifer has admitted that her imagination often runs away with her – and that she would love to see the *Ab Fab* movie nominated for an Academy Award one day. 'I'll do it so that Patsy and Eddy can walk the red carpet,' she said.

'Wouldn't that be a dream?'

An Oscar for Jennifer Saunders? Why ever not? She might not be crazy about the idea of having to get seriously dressed up for Tinseltown's premier bash – Eddy would adore all those designers and stylists clamouring for her attention but her creator might prefer to stick to the low-key, more discreet glamour that has become her trademark. And maybe when she walks up onto the stage and the whole world watches as Jennifer makes that acceptance speech, it will be fairly brief and to the point.

But you can bet your life it will be funny.

Because, essentially, all you really need to know about the legendary and outrageously talented Jennifer Saunders is this: she knows how to make us laugh. And she's fair set to keep on doing just that for many moons to come.

So Viva Jennifer. Forever...